D0396842

God Has a Story Too

GOD HAS A STORY TOO

SERMONS IN CONTEXT

James A. Sanders

FORTRESS PRESS   Philadelphia

The permission granted by the following publishers is hereby gratefully acknowledged: *Union Seminary Quarterly Review* for the sermon "Promise and Providence" in chapter 1, the sermon "Banquet of the Dispossessed" in chapter 5, the sermon "In the Same Night . . ." in chapter 6, and the sermon "Outside the Camp" in chapter 7; the Ministers and Missionaries Benefit Board of the American Baptist Churches for the sermon "The New History: Joseph Our Brother" in chapter 2; Thesis Creative Educational Resources for the sermon "What Happened at Nazareth?" in chapter 4, and the sermon "Banquet of the Dispossessed" in chapter 5; Colgate Rochester Divinity School for the sermon "It Is Finished" in chapter 8.

Library of Congress Cataloging in Publication Data

Sanders, James A   1927–
  God has a story too.

  Includes bibliographical references and index.
  1. Sermons, American. 2. Presbyterian Church.
3. Bible—Hermeneutics. 4. Preaching. I. Title.
BX9178.S28G62   252′.05′1   77-15244
ISBN 0-8006-1353-8

For Sisters Agnes and Iris and my sister, Nell,
women who told me the tomb was empty,
and
for Ruth and Joe Brown Love,
who told me my head need not be

Contents

Preface

This volume is a response to requests to provide copies of some of the sermons I have preached in the churches. It is about the importance of seeing and hearing texts in specific contexts in order to understand the original points they might have scored as well as the points they have scored in later contexts. Each sermon is prefaced by a description of the situation in which it was first preached. Also, each sermon is given here in its original first-draft form. This last point has caused me some pain, for in preaching some of the sermons more than once I have from one occasion to the next improved and polished them considerably. But it would miss altogether the point of what I want to do in this volume if I were to publish here a later form instead of the sermon first heard in the context described.

I beg forgiveness right away of all readers for the sexist language in some of the pieces. Some date back almost twenty years. Until a few years ago I had not had my consciousness raised about the sexist language we all were using. Our minds in the fifties, sixties, and even early seventies were focused on other theological and social problems. But if I were to abide by the decision to use the first draft of each, for the reasons given above, I could not begin to edit the manuscripts for any reason or I would abandon the purpose of the volume. Some of the later pieces show improvement, I hope. I continue to learn.

The dedication wants a word of explanation. While I was working on getting the book together I received a letter from Mrs. Iris Masserano of Bethel Assembly, Inc., in Memphis, Tennessee, my home town. In it she mentioned that she had seen a copy of an interview article published in the *Kansas City Star* in January of 1977 when I had been lecturing for a week at the Village Presbyterian Church in Prairie Village, Kansas. Then she wrote, "First let me identify myself. I am Iris of the Agnes and Iris team." That sentence spanned a gap of forty years.

I had mentioned to the *Star* journalist, who asked about the current charismatic movement, that I was "saved" in the First Assembly of God Church in Memphis at the age of six during services conducted there by a team of evangelists, Agnes and Iris. Sister Agnes, now Mrs. William Lewis of Watson, Illinois, apparently saw the article first and sent a copy to Sister Iris. How well I remember them in their long satin dresses. Sister Iris played the guitar and Sister Agnes preached. Paul and Silas were in jail in Philippi, but the prison bars broke that night in Memphis not only for them but for me. I hope my intellectual friends and colleagues take no offense at this public report of that occasion. For many years I never mentioned it, but I never forgot it. It too is a part of what is here. The least that might be said is that the so-called charismatic movement is not a recent phenomenon; it has been there all along in the blue-collar churches as well as the black churches.

In the same letter Sister Iris wrote, "I would like to ask you, in case you want to take time to answer this letter, if you have a sister whose name is Nell?" It was Nell who had taken little brother to services that night in Memphis and who on occasion assisted Agnes and Iris in those services. I can remember the four of us traveling across town in a beat-up old car going from one meeting to another, singing gospel songs. Our journeys were punctuated by the hope that no officer would stop us because of a darkened taillight or a muffler needing to be replaced—for which there was no money. But the spirit fairly soared on such occasions: we were in other hands.

Nell died in 1972 in an automobile accident in Memphis. But my spiritual indebtedness to those three women is as great as it is to Mary Magdalene, Joanna, Mary, the Mother of James, and the others (Luke 24:10), the spice and news bearers, witnesses of dazzling apparel.

And my gratitude is just as great to two others, Ruth and Joe Brown Love, who twelve years later provided a kind of second saving experience. I was an undergraduate at Vanderbilt University where they had come from the University of Illinois to head the Wesley Foundation in Nashville. Over a period of time, and by gentle suasion, they convinced me that one's intelligence as well as one's emotion could be put to the service of faith. Nobody had actually told that to me in the way they did. I did not hide the fact that I loved study and made mostly A's, but one simply did not mention it—that was something one did on the side almost, hoping it would not affect one's religion. There was an unspoken assumption that intellect and religion were opposed to each other in a sort of ongoing Scopes Trial of the mind against the heart. The Loves opened to me a whole new world of personal integrity of mind and heart—so much so that to this day I have difficulty understanding the dichotomy some of my colleagues feel between preaching and scholarship. The Loves showed me the marriage of ecclesia and academia: to be in the one does not necessarily mean denial of the other.

God bless them all, and grant them long life and strength to enjoy it.

Introduction: Contextual Hermeneutics in Biblical Preaching

Something to Say

In May 1971 at the tenth anniversary meeting in Denver of the Consultation on Church Union, Peter Berger issued a call to the churches that they too have something to say.[1] Ecumenism had by that time begun to address itself to the question of missiology —a renewed understanding of the mission of Christianity in the light both of pluralism and of the recent expressions of individualistic spirituality, the so-called charismatic movement.

Pluralism had brought the churches to a genuine appreciation of the need to find ways of hearing and affirming the voice of God through other than Christian sources in his broad creation. Berger fully supported this appreciation but stressed that in their dialogues with other faiths and with "isms" the churches too have something to say: the very raison d'être of their existence, the Christian story.

The charismatic movement had led and was leading many Christians so to stress their own individual stories, or testimonies, that there was the danger of losing sight of the community grounding of Christian experience. As so often in the past century or more, so-called liberals and so-called fundamentalists have been expressing very similar concerns, each using, however, quite different idioms by which to do so. The current charismatic movement finds its liberal expression in the recital of private, personal experiences such as those familiar in the writings of Sam Keen, Harvey Cox, Malcolm Boyd, Tom Driver, William Coffin, and others.[2] This too is a part of the current emphasis on the Holy Spirit as a reaction against the earlier "neoorthodox" stress on the Word. Such shifts in emphasis have taken place throughout the history of Christian theology.[3] To emphasize personal experience as a principal ground for theologizing is to stress

1

the pervasive work of the Holy Spirit (even in the liberal guise of either denying or celebrating the work of inner demons).

What follows is in no wise intended to denigrate either pluralism or the charismatic movement in their several current manifestations. It is an effort however to say clearly, with Peter Berger and others, that we have a common story even within the current contexts of pluralism on the one hand and private charismata on the other. God has a story too; and it is his story which is our real purpose in being. It is God's story in Torah and in Christ which is gospel for the Christian. Those private stories which show it forth in varied and even surprising ways are precious indeed— and woe be unto any church body or person that would stifle its emergence in ever new and challenging forms.

An integral part of the concept of gospel, or God's story, however, is the freedom of God's grace, the *opus alienum* which challenges all forms of denominationalism and individualism. Interesting in Denver was the liberal reaction at the conference to Berger's statement. Many there heard him in terms of an older, pervasive dichotomy that has plagued Christianity perhaps since its inception, that of emphasis on celebrating the gospel (God's work) as the principal mission and work of the churches, and of emphasis on shaping society in the light thereof (obedience, or human works). Many Western Christians have the strange notion that to engage in either of these is somehow to devalue the other. Some Christians apparently feel that the whole mission of the churches is to preach the gospel to all nations, while others apparently feel that to do so in certain ways is part of the fundamentalist heresy. And some in Denver argued with Berger past midnight on the day of his speech to the effect that his call to remembrance of the Christian story would have the effect of stressing preaching and reducing the churches' commitments to social reform.

If the writer may be permitted to indulge his own story a moment, it is in part because of this strange dichotomy in Western Christian thinking that he became, while on the faculty of Union Theological Seminary in New York, an affiliate member, "under watch-care," of the Concord Baptist Church of Christ in Brooklyn. Black churches generally, and that church in particular, do not suffer the dichotomy. Gardner Taylor, the pastor, Sunday after Sunday preaches and celebrates the gospel with both intellectual content and unabashed enthusiasm with no dichotomy sensed or expressed between gospel and social action. One fires and feeds the other; they go together, they belong together. Western Christians, liberal and conservative, need to hear Peter Berger, Gardner Taylor, and others who are not burdened by such false dichotomies.

Occasionally I am invited by the Office of General Assembly of the United Presbyterian Church in the U.S.A., my denomination, to function in certain situations as a sort of honorary consultant on biblical affairs, so to speak. These have usually been those occasions when the office would invite the liberal and conservative groups of the church for debate and conversation largely with an aim toward reconciliation between them. One can sit and listen to such conversations and easily get the impression that one might be auditing debates within Western churches at most any point in church history. There have always been those who have felt that the main mission of the church was to celebrate the gospel—one way or another—as well as those who have felt that the main mission of the church was to help shape society in the light thereof. If the Torah-Christ story, God's story, is made up of the two principal elements *muthos* and *ethos* (gospel and law, *haggadah and halachah*),[4] then throughout church history God seems to have provided himself in every age with those who have stressed the one as well as with those who have stressed the other. The unfortunate thing has been the tendency in each group, conservative and liberal, throughout the centuries to think their emphasis was the right one. I have attempted from time to time to gauge which of them within the Presbyterian Church seemed the more arrogant about their conviction, but I have never been able to decide; both seem quite confident. One point in all this is certain: never in the history of the Christian church has individualism—whether in terms of personal story or personal piety, whether liberal or conservative— had any significant meaning apart from grounding in and challenge from the fuller gospel of the canon from Genesis through the New Testament.

In quite another vein, what follows is in part recognition and appreciation of the work of two scholars published in 1973. Far from being an adequate response to them this collection of sermons in context is for me nonetheless a way of identifying with their concern. They both presented dynamic modes of understanding biblical thinking in terms of contemporary political and philosophic problems. And each called for working out a history or biography of God.

George Mendenhall argued eloquently for understanding early biblical traditions as having been hammered out in the tough political arenas of the Near East in the Bronze and Iron Ages.[5] Israel's self-understanding was forged in the realities of numerous successive power-flows in antiquity from one political base to another, from the Egyptian to the Assyrian to the Babylonian to the Persian to the Greek to the Roman. This flow occurred roughly every tenth generation and produced anxiety and destruction in its path. The Bible includes the record of the efforts of thinkers in Israel to perceive the work of God in the midst of these flows and what might otherwise be called meaningless evil. One of Mendenhall's chapters (VIII) is titled "Toward a Biography of God: Religion and Politics as Reciprocals." Mendenhall does not attempt himself to write the biography but indicates that the Bible would be the principal resource for it.

James Barr in the same year and without collusion sounded a similar note, commenting on what he calls the popular view of a static God who "by the mere fact of being God cannot say anything imperfect, just as they think he cannot change." In a brilliant footnote, easily overlooked, he added: "This completely static view of God is in conflict with the biblical insistence on the living God; it makes it difficult for people to see theological significance in what happens in the world; and it is a major obstacle to the appreciation of the Bible in any modern categories. Against this static view it is preferable to say, even at the risk of being misunderstood, that God has a history—though, naturally, not identical with human history."[6] Barr calls for a view of inspiration that would have "nothing to do with inerrancy or infallibility" but would apply to the formation of tradition that finally comprised Scripture rather than to the formation of Scripture.[7]

God has a story too. What follows is a way of looking at the
story in ancient contexts and a way of retelling the story in
modern contexts.

Text and Context

Biblical preaching in context means re-presenting today the
message of a biblical passage for the contemporary context, scor-
ing as closely as possible for the modern hearer the point or
points scored originally by the biblical authors and thinkers in
their time. Stable as it is, the Bible itself presupposes and suggests such adaptability. It is the nature of the Bible as canon to
be adaptable to the situations and concerns of the ongoing believing communities who find their identity in the biblical story.
However, the Bible as canon also has stability. Though Jewish,
Roman Catholic, Orthodox, and Protestant canons vary, the canon
within any particular communion has a certain number of books
or writings. And the text of a canon also has some stability despite
the vast number of variants among the ancient manuscripts which
record the Bible in its original languages and early translations.
Indeed, the concept of canon is located in the tension between
two poles, stability and adaptability, with hermeneutics as the
mid-term between them.

Adapt-	Herme-	Sta-
ability	neutics	bility

Whereas the various biblical communions, Jewish and Christian, may differ on what is in and what is out of their several
canons, they all agree, liberal and conservative alike, that the
content of the canon, and even to a certain limited degree the
form of it, is adaptable to the essential and existential concerns
of the communities whose identities depend on it and who trans-
mit it generation by generation from parents to children. The
Bible is relevant. On that point there is no disagreement among
any of the peoples of the book! On the point of how to adapt it
and what that adaptation may signify, however, there is considerable pluralism.

The Bible's ongoing adaptability is due to three major factors.

The first of these is its pluralism. Since it encompasses in its writings some fifteen hundred years of struggle with the questions of faith expressed in numerous idioms spanning five ancient culture eras (Bronze Age, Iron Age, Persian Age, Hellenistic, and Roman) and covering the full gamut of problems a people might face trying to know who they were and what they should do in everchanging circumstances, it is understandably pluralistic. At no point was it filtered through the necessarily limited thinking of a single synagogue or church council.[8] It is full of contrapositives. It has limits, to be sure, but those limits were not superimposed on it at some theological bottleneck in antiquity by a council or councils. Its limits and its shape are defined by factors which were operative in the reality of life spun out in ancient Israel and in early Judaism, but not by the focused theological concerns of one generation sitting in the midst of a single set of problems. It is limited by the fact that all the literature in it comes from the eastern half of the ancient Mediterranean world: there is no clear tradition in it stemming directly from Southwest Africa or the Far East, for instance. But within its bounds it is pluralistic enough to be adaptable to life even in such places as those.

The second major factor in the Bible's adaptability is its inherent ambiguity. Like good poetry its literature has depths and levels. Even those portions directed and aimed originally at very specific concerns in a single time-space setting have been adaptable to other contexts. Words Jeremiah spoke in the seventh century in Judah before the fall of Jerusalem said something quite different to Jews in exile in the sixth.[9] Jesus' prophetic critique of his fellow Jews in the first third of the first century may have sounded to the young uncertain churches in the last third of the century like an absolute denial of Jewish claims to being the people of God—something Jesus never said, any more than did Amos or Jeremiah in earlier contexts.

What ended up in the Bible, even small literary units in some cases, had to be able to speak to more than one group at one time and to differing contexts in the following generations. Otherwise we would simply not have inherited it but would perhaps be discovering it by archaeology in caves or holes in the ground in the Near East. We have to remember that the "new" literature discovered by archaeologists in modern times is in reality ancient literature which simply did not "make it." Either the community which produced it did not survive, or there came a point where it simply did not span the next generation gap and was not passed on.[10] Canonical literature by contrast "made it," and not only early on—it has continued to offer value to succeeding generations of those who receive it. For that to happen in the first generations or centuries after composition there must have been, besides inherent value, some built-in ambiguity sufficient to permit it to speak to differing needs, groups, and contexts. As James Barr says, "It is the shape of the tradition that leads Jesus to the findings of his obedience; but it is also the shape of the tradition that leads his enemies to see him as a blasphemer and to demand that he should be put to death. . . . The tradition works . . . not only to illuminate and to identify the Christ, but also to reject and resist the Christ."[11]

After a certain point, when the literature attained some measure of communal sanctity, there entered into the tradition of that literature (book or group of books) the conviction that it would thereafter always be relevant, whether or not it seemed so at first blush. At that point it was a valid candidate for canonicity and there arose the third major factor in the Bible's adaptability, hermeneutics.

Actually, whenever a text intended for one context is applied to another or different context some kind of hermeneutics is necessary to adapt the text to the new situation. Even the uninformed who think they are simply being "faithful to the text" when they seek to read it "accurately" are nonetheless using hermeneutics, if for no other reason than the fact that they are of necessity using their own minds in reading the text. How can they do otherwise? And those minds are of necessity shaped by the culture in which they were nurtured. One of the important features of Bible study today is that of becoming conscious, in the churches as well as in seminaries and universities, of what hermeneutics one is using when reading a text. One purpose of this collection of sermons is to aid in that process.

Hermeneutics is of two main sorts. One involves the exegetic tools which have been developed by biblical scholars over the

past two centuries in order to recover points originally scored in
Bible times by the biblical authors and theologians themselves.
These are the "principles, rules, and techniques whereby the interpreter of a text attempts to understand it in its original context."[12]
These include all the biblical "criticisms"—text criticism, source
criticism, form criticism, tradition criticism, redaction criticism,
and canonical criticism—as well as philology and archaeology.
These tools have been developed and honed over the past two
hundred years and continue to develop. They are focused on both
the ancient text and the ancient context.

That meaning, however, is not the one most people have in
mind when they speak today of hermeneutics. When one hears
the term today, outside of such strictly defined Old Testament or
New Testament exegetical settings as a seminary class or a meeting of Bible scholars, it usually refers to the second main sort of
hermeneutics: those means used to translate a thought or event
from one cultural context (from an ancient text) to another (our
modern times). This is a sane and sage recognition of the fact
that both the ancient writer and the modern interpreter are con-
ditioned by the cultures in which they lived or live. There has to
be some kind of conversion key, as it were, to bring the one over
into the other if the integrity of the text is to be honored and
somehow preserved, and if that text is to be heard at all by the
modern listener.

First, then, we try to understand the text in its original context;
that requires scientific, exegetic tools of the first sort of hermeneutics. Then we try to understand it in our own context; that is the
second sort. The number of people with the expertise to do the
former is somewhat limited. But the fruit of their labors is available in books and commentaries published by denominational and
secular publishing houses. Part of the reason the churches are
asked to support their seminaries in modern times is to support
the trained scholars who often teach in those seminaries so that
they can do the research and publishing necessary to make that
expertise available to the pastors, teachers, and layfolk in the
churches.

There are not many people abroad who can engage equally
well in both sorts of hermeneutics. Indeed, there is a widespread

attitude of dichotomy among both scholars and interpreters which causes people to assume that no one person can do both. When a biblical scholar is invited to speak in a church setting one of the deep concerns of the pastor is whether the scholar will really be able to speak to the people. Will he or she use words too difficult for them, or concepts they cannot grasp—or indeed concepts offensive to the faithful? On the other hand, when an interpreter has developed a certain repute as being helpful in the churches it is tacitly assumed on the part of Bible scholars that he has abandoned scholarship. Those of us who do technical, highly academic scholarship and also go into the churches and turn people on to the Bible as we perceive it are apparently not quite credible to either group: we have to keep doing both to prove ourselves. Sometimes it is a bit annoying to have to fight the prejudice, but it is always a joy when it is overcome in actual experience with either group. My good friends in the churches who may benefit from the present effort may not know the kind of prejudice one will face in the scholarly guilds when it is learned that one has published "a book of sermons." Scholars have their biases too!

In part because of such dichotomy of thinking Bible scholars have sometimes left the second sort of hermeneutics to folk outside their professional guild. A notable exception has been Rudolf Bultmann, a great New Testament scholar who has spent a great deal of his professional life developing the second sort of hermeneutics. A good many of his students and grand-students have continued his work, agreeing with him and disagreeing with him, trying to work out valid modern enlightenment modes of hermeneutics whereby to render the New Testament messages potent and pertinent today. But aside from such efforts on the part of some Bible scholars most work of the second sort has been done by philosophers and theologians. And all of them tend to import their hermeneutics to the Bible from modern thought forms. There has been some confusion, therefore, between hermeneutics—the means of converting ancient thoughts to contemporary thought forms—and those contemporary thought forms which receive the ancient.

Just as linguists speak of modern "receptor languages" into which ancient texts are translated, so we can speak of modern "receptor thought forms" into which ancient thought forms are rendered by hermeneutics. It is in part the thesis of this book that a valid hermeneutic we might use in interpreting the Bible today can be derived from the biblical experience itself, and not imported from the outside.

The first sort of hermeneutics of which we have spoken, the scholarly tools developed over the past two hundred years which help us recover the points originally scored back in biblical times, has now reached the point in its own development that we are able, to a greater or lesser degree, depending on the passage involved, to recover not only the original points scored but in many cases to recover the hermeneutics used by the biblical thinkers and authors! This was not possible until the development of modern biblical criticism, and even then has become feasible only in very recent times as biblical criticism has improved its tools. Those tools continue to need experimentation and improvement. And at times they fail us. They especially fail us when they become ends in themselves. But they provide us now with the possibility of recovering, in many passages, the hermeneutics used in antiquity when still more ancient traditions were contemporized.

One of the most fruitful newer emphases in biblical study is to begin work on a biblical passage by locating in it citations from or allusions to older traditions which the author called on in advancing his own argument or theme. Sometimes in a New Testament passage there are rather full citations of an Old Testament passage, but often the text has been modified and altered by the New Testament author to suit his or her argument. Sometimes the New Testament author simply used a text of the Old Testament different from those we have, but more often than not the later author actually adapted the older text to the new purposes. Sometimes the later author simply wove Old Testament traditions into the argument by using familiar Old Testament phrases or themes or ideas.[13] Once such references have been identified, then one begins work on *how* the later author adapted them and made the Old Testament tradition relevant to problems in the early churches. Such re-presentation of older traditions begins of course way back in Old Testament times. Most Jewish literature dating from after the middle of the sixth century B.C.E.

was composed in the terms and accents of older traditions. To recover the hermeneutics employed by the biblical author on the tradition cited or alluded to we need to know as much as possible about the ancient context for which the author was writing so as to reconstruct as nearly as possible the concerns of the congregation or community among whom or for whom the author wrote. This is not always possible, and where possible is rarely precise. But there are tools for doing so and they are improving.

The Bible is full of such unrecorded hermeneutics because it is itself so full of re-presented tradition. New Testament study has until recently tended to pay minimal attention to the Old Testament in the New. For some students there seemed to be regret over the amount of good New Testament space taken up and lost in quoting the Old. It was part of the centuries-long Christian conviction in many quarters that the New Testament had superseded the Old. Now we realize what a mine of information can be gained by focusing attention, initially, on the hermeneutic question of an ancient text. A question some of us are asking is whether such unrecorded biblical hermeneutics may not be as important for the churches and synagogues today as anything expressly stated in the Bible. The answer to that question depends in part on one's view of the ontology of the Bible, its nature. If one views the Bible primarily as a source of wisdom, a casket of ancient gems still negotiable today, then the answer is likely to be no. But if one views the Bible primarily as a paradigm, to be applied dynamically to modern idioms and verbs, then the answer is quite likely to be yes, for then we want to learn how they back there, right in the canonical literature itself, dynamically applied their own prior traditions to their day.

The question might arise at this point as to why we should go to all the trouble of recovering the points they scored back then. Is it not the nature of canon, as we say, to be adaptable, and if so why can we not just read it directly for ourselves without bothering to find out how it functioned or what it said specifically back then? There are some very wise and sane people who are saying this today.[14] There is a new group of biblical interpreters who call themselves structuralists.[15] They disdain the use of biblical criticism and focus on the overall structure of a biblical passage no matter when or how it was first composed, or for what purpose. One might rightly point out that the biblical authors themselves did not rehash the original meaning of the traditions or scripture they cited; usually they simply interpreted the tradition quite directly for their own time. There are interesting exceptions,[16] but for the most part the biblical authors sought value in the tradition directly rather than recovering the points it first scored and then applying those points to their time.[17]

It is generally a trait of our post-Enlightenment era to seek original points of traditional material. In fact, it is quite possible to think that biblical criticism has gone too far in its tendency to find authority only in the most primitive meaning of a passage; in this respect it has been a bit antiquarian.[18] Canonical criticism has opened the way to understand the pluralism of how a single tradition may have as many different meanings as there are allusions to it or citations of it in the Bible itself—and how the most primitive is not the only authoritative one.[19]

But neither is the meaning we may discern out of our immediate modern contexts the only authoritative one. On the contrary, unless there are firm exegetic controls applied in reading a text, it is possible that we might never hear what Jeremiah or Jesus said, or what their first hearers understood them to say. The points originally scored by the biblical thinkers and authors gave rise to the very process of preservation of the biblical materials we inherit. No one started out to write a biblical book with such authority that it would be accepted by the several early believing communities. What the original thinker said must have been valuable enough to be remembered and then passed on. We are sophisticated enough to know that what a person intended to communicate and what was heard and understood even by those immediately present may be two quite different things. Then of course the reasons for preserving the material and the reasons the first subsequent generation also found it valuable may have been quite different. What Baruch understood Jeremiah to say in Jerusalem before the Temple fell and what the exiles understood a repetition of his message to mean for them a decade or two later may have been quite different. The factor of context in understanding a text is very important indeed. In fact, recognition of the factor of modern context in reading an ancient text is important if we want to recover the points originally scored. We need to be aware of our own needs and what they do to us when we formulate our questions to pose to an ancient text.

Even scholars, or especially scholars, need to be aware of their own limitations in this regard. A cursory review of the history of biblical criticism in the past two hundred years is informative in this regard. We can now see how the questions which interested scholars in the eighteenth century, or in the nineteenth century, or early in the twentieth, influenced the way they saw a text. Knowledge of such a history of shifting interest and method in scholarly work raises our own consciousness as to what questions we are now asking and makes us aware of the methods we are using. We have only recently been released from the almost unconscious hermeneutic of evolutionism. Interest in this sort of self-criticism has arisen only recently, parallel to the new discipline called the sociology of knowledge. One observation which results from such a review of the past two hundred years is that modern scholarship has lines of continuity with earlier pre-Enlightenment scholarship: We are all human and subject to the Zeitgeist of our times. Another observation such a review affords is that each generation in one way or another felt that it had a special claim on truth, that history was to some degree culminating in its work. With the new sociology of knowledge, and in part because of it, we are in danger of thinking that we are liberated from the earlier tendencies and that we truly have a corner on truth! That is the Catch-22 aspect of intellectual endeavor.

We can all read into a text what we need to find there. Biblical criticism at its best, employed circumspectly, is the best means of avoiding abuse of the Bible. For all our observations that we are all human, scholarship has developed tools over the past two hundred years that can help us recover, to a good degree of probability, the thoughts and understandings of ancient folk. And there is perhaps no field of literary scholarship that is more scrupulously circumspect than biblical criticism. Most folk engaged in it have their identity in some modern denominational form of its traditions (Jewish, Muslim, or Christian), and most of us are extra careful in this regard, more so perhaps than when we work on Ugaritic literature or Homer or Herodotus. Indeed, the reaction of some people in the churches and in theology is that we have been too scrupulous: with our methods and tools we have tended to lock the Bible into the past, we have become antiquarian.

Even so the tools developed are very valuable and can now be employed to recover the points originally scored within the biblical orbit (that is, the understandings of a "text" not only when first spoken or written but also in the generations and contexts immediately following, within the range of biblical history). It is only by so doing that we can also recover the hermeneutics of the biblical authors and thinkers themselves. Anytime they contemporized a tradition in their time, they used hermeneutics. The time has now arrived in biblical scholarship to work on those hermeneutics; and we can do so only by using all the tools of biblical scholarship to gauge how the more ancient texts functioned in the less ancient contexts. That requires discerning the ancient contexts and the needs of the earliest believing communities who heard the actual biblical thinkers as much as it requires discerning the ancient texts. We must work not only on biblical literary criticism (source criticism, form criticism, tradition criticism, redaction criticism) but also on biblical historical criticism (philology, archaeology, history of religions, anthropology, secular historiography). We must work not only on text but on context. And if we do so we can then begin to discern these unrecorded hermeneutics latent throughout the Bible. The literature available on internal biblical hermeneutics is not yet very large, but it is growing.[20]

Hermeneutics is theology and theology is hermeneutics. The wisdom of this very old observation is almost immediately and directly applicable to study of biblical or canonical hermeneutics. That is, the deciding light in which one reads a passage is determined by the reader's operative view of God or, to use Dietrich Bonhoeffer's term, of reality, or if one prefers, of truth. And one's view of God tends to emphasize either God's freedom or God's commitment to promises made in a covenantal pact issuing from and out of some great redemptive act (such as the Exodus event or the Christ event). The latter is called divine grace.

On the one hand tradition has always maintained that God is God and hence free to create new factors in the human situation and pull surprises even on his own elect people. John Calvin called this aspect of God's work *opera aliena* (from Isa. 28:21): God is free to follow his own agenda which may surprise even his most faithful adherents. God's freedom is inherent in his role as Creator, which is an ongoing role and was not abandoned after Creation. On the other hand God's function as Redeemer emphasizes God's faithfulness to promises made either to the elect-redeemed or to all creation or to both. God's grace then stresses his reliability and long-suffering.

The hermeneutic of God's freedom as Creator of all the world and of all humankind may be called the hermeneutic of prophetic critique. The hermeneutic of God's grace and commitment to the promises made as the peculiar and particular Redeemer of one ongoing community or group may be called constitutive hermeneutics. The one hermeneutic stresses God's role as Creator of all and the other tends to emphasize God's role as Redeemer of a particular group; the one focuses on the doctrine of creation and the other on the doctrine of redemption. Other doctrines or views tend to be colored by which of these two one stresses, and the history of Christian thought seems to alternate between stress on the one and emphasis on the other. The doctrines of election, ecclesiology, providence, and eschatology may be colored by whether one focuses on God as universal Sovereign of all or on God as Redeemer of a particular group. The one hermeneutic is theocentric, the other christocentric.

Actually, part of the Bible's pluralism is seen in its ability to hold these two emphases in tension. One may employ the most sophisticated tools of biblical criticism to see how Genesis 1 came from one ancient source and Genesis 2 from another. Such an observation helps to understand the apparent contradictions between the two chapters—how, for instance, humanity was created last according to Genesis 1 but was created first according to Genesis 2. So far so good. But it is also very important to observe that some good editor wisely put the two chapters, despite such obvious discrepancies, back to back. And he was supported in that juxtaposition by subsequent believing communities who accepted his work and passed it along as valuable. (This last is a canonical-critical observation.) What then do the two chapters say back to back? They say that God is both majestically transcendent and humbly immanent: neither view of God excludes the other. Traditionally, holding two such opposing views at the same time is called a paradox. But it is very important to observe that the Bible presents these two pictures of God—majestically creating the world by divine fiat *and* calling on Adam and Eve like a pastor—rather constantly throughout. In fact one could say they keep reappearing in alternating cadences.

All efforts to combine the two and mix them so as to view God as a sort of majestic pastor seem to fail. On the contrary the canon as a whole consists of literary units, small and large, some of which almost exclusively stress the one (Ecclesiastes, say) or the other (the Gospel of John). That is the reason the word *paradox* has been used. Other efforts to stress one to the exclusion of the other also fail. To press an exclusivist christocentric or redemptional view of God runs the danger of denominational hermeneutics: God is our God because he did such and such for us and made us promises he made nobody else, so everybody had best join our church. Or it runs the danger of so stressing divine forgiveness and grace that ethics loses ground altogether. Blessed assurance is absolutely right in Christian doctrine (and Jewish, for that matter); but if it stands alone, out of tension with God's freedom to judge his own people, it becomes cheap grace, or what a student once called sloppy agape. On the other hand to press an inclusivist theocentric view of God as universal sovereign of all peoples, unfettered by any expectation of how he might act, runs the danger of the view that God is but whimsical and unreliable; ethics loses ground here also.

Holding the two in tension, not attempting either to opt absolutely and always for the one or the other, or to mix them into a neat fifty-fifty formula, seems to be what the Bible does. The reason is that in some contexts or situations in which the believing communities found themselves they needed to hear the challenge of God's freedom, and in other contexts they needed to hear the comfort of God's grace. This is what is meant by the ancient assertion that God's Word comforts the afflicted and afflicts the

comfortable. Falsehood enters in when a biblical passage or ancient tradition is brought to bear upon a context where it could
either comfort cruel people (by stressing God's grace when they
needed to hear a challenge) or quench a dimly burning wick (by
stressing God's freedom when they needed to hear of comfort and
support). Any passage, actually, can be interpreted either way
according to the hermeneutic employed—either the hermeneutic
of prophetic critique stressing for that context and for that reading God's freedom, or the hermeneutic of constitutive support
stressing for that context and for that reading God's grace.

The following diagram suggests the dynamics of the triangular
process whereby text and context are brought together by way of
a hermeneutic that is either prophetic or constitutive, depending
on whether stress falls on the freedom of God or on the grace
of God:

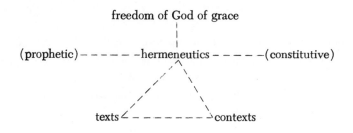

Biblical Hermeneutics

The sermons which follow reflect to a greater or lesser degree
some of the biblical hermeneutics we have been recovering from
working in this manner on the Bible. I shall not attempt here to
describe all that work. Rather I would like to describe the hermeneutics which, inspired by that work, I myself used in developing the meaning of a particular passage for a particular modern
context. Preceding each sermon is a short description of the context for which the sermon was originally composed, so that readers can discern for themselves, from where they are now, sitting
and reading this book, as nearly as possible what might have
taken place when I first preached it. In other words, I do here
what I dearly wish the ancient biblical authors had also done:

make clear the particular, limited needs I saw in each case and the intention I had in attempting to meet them.

Here I simply want to describe the basic thrust of the hermeneutics I employ when I sit with a text to render it pertinent to our day.

First of all, I nearly always employ prophetic hermeneutics.[21] Prophetic hermeneutics stresses particularly the freedom of God. Nearly all my preaching is done by invitation in white, male-dominated churches which form part of the dominant, established culture of this country. The pews are often filled with people who have some political and financial clout and who perhaps need to have their consciousness raised on how that clout affects others. The fact that those churches are in the United States of America means that they are a part of the richest nation the world has ever known. From the standpoint of ancient Judea as much as from the viewpoint of workers and peasants in Brazil or Chile, Kenya or India, we are the rich. Any biblically derived hermeneutic must avoid so applying the text as either to comfort cruel people or hurt the weak. But our people are not cruel, we say! Of course not. Neither did Ramses II consider himself cruel, or Nebuchadnezzar, or Herod, or the Roman troops. All had jobs to do and all probably compared themselves only with other people having similar responsibilities.

Prophetic hermeneutics means, therefore, that we read a text so as to see the full humanity and position of those who otherwise appear to be "bad guys" (or "gals"). Prophetic hermeneutics means not so much comforting the afflicted as afflicting the comfortable. It means applying a text sociologically and politically to a situation today in which we are involved, just as the prophets in like manner applied the traditions they inherited to ancient Israel and ancient Judah, and as Jesus in large measure did in his day. The text or tradition is applied as a challenge.

Prophetic hermeneutics on the other hand—and we have to be clear about this—is not for use in pastoral counseling. It is not normally for individual application. There is plenty in the Bible that may be used in pastoral care with the bereaved, the suffering, the mentally disturbed, the emotionally upset, those in need of marriage counseling, but it is not to be found in the prophets—

not without extremely careful application of a kind of hermeneutics which will not be discussed here at all. But why use an Amos, for instance, in individual counseling when there is so much else in the Bible? The book of Job stands as a loud no against using prophetic theology in dealing with an individual who is suffering beyond all possible notions of justice. Job's friends tried to apply the thinking of Hosea, Jeremiah, and Deuteronomy to Job's personal problems—and with disastrous results! It simply should not be done. There is in the Bible enough humanitarian wisdom tradition for individual application without trying to make Isaiah apply to someone's private pain, or joy.[22]

Very seldom am I invited to preach in situations where constitutive or supportive hermeneutics, stressing God's grace or absolute commitment, would be pertinent. Dr. Gardner Taylor has three times had me preach at the Concord Baptist Church of Christ (where I am an affiliate member) in Bedford-Stuyvesant in Brooklyn. Each time I had to work very hard to apply a constitutive hermeneutic: I am not used to it. It would be totally impertinent for me, a white man, to preach a seriously challenging sermon in that church. Gardner Taylor does so with tremendous effect. But that is because a prophet always arises out of his or her own people and cannot be a "visiting fireman." He loves them and they love him, deeply. So I have tried there instead to preach in such a way as not to quench a dimly burning wick but to encourage the people to know the fellowship of Christ when they return to whitey's factory or kitchen or garbage dump on Monday.

But none of that effort is here. In the sermons of this book I try to get whitey, myself and my brother and sister in the fine suburban situation, to take Ramses, Sennacherib, Herod, and Pilate as mirrors to see what it is we do to others when we do not even know we are doing it, bless us. I preach with love. I identify with the congregation. I want us to hear the challenge of Hosea and Jesus, or even of Genesis and Kings, the blessing in store for us if we try. In the biblical literature it was the responsible folk, those on top of the social and political pile, who were those most like us now. If we continue to view them as bad guys, we'll never feel the piercing two-edged sword the Word can be. In this regard we need simply to be good historians. The Pharisees were good guys by any standard we can apply. They were the responsible religious folk of Jesus' day who tried hard to be obedient and live lives pleasing to God. We can learn much from our Jewish neighbors today, the contemporary heirs of Pharisaic Judaism, about how good they really were.

Once we are convinced of that and permit ourselves psychologically to identify a bit with them, then hear Jesus' prophetic challenges to them, his fellow Jews—at that point and at that point only will we hear the poignancy of what Jesus was saying to them. To continue to identify with Jeremiah and Jesus in our reading of them is to continue the evil and falsehood of anti-Semitism. If we read Amos or Jeremiah out of context they sound anti-Semitic. To continue to read the New Testament—especially the Gospels—out of context is to see it as anti-Semitic. Prophets identified with their people and loved them even while they challenged them. That is the reason "no prophet is acceptable in his own country" (Luke 4:24). The prophets revealed the secrets of the hearts of their people, as Simeon said Christ would do (Luke 2:35). And Christ did, but we can make him sound anti-Semitic if we read the Gospels out of original context.

So one of the first hermeneutic techniques we can use to employ prophetic critique in application of a text is dynamic analogy. We should look for the persons and figures in it who might represent different folk today dynamically. Dynamic analogy means we can read a text in different ways by identifying with different people in it. For example if we always identify with Jesus in the passage in Luke 4, his sermon at Nazareth, then we will read the last verse of the pericope (Luke 4:30) wondering how Jesus managed to escape that awful crowd. How marvelous! But if we read the passage again, identifying with the good folk in the synagogue, Jesus' relatives and friends of his hometown, and see how he so sorely offended them that they tried to lynch him, then by the time we get to verse 30 we ask an entirely different question: How did the scoundrel get away?

That is far from blasphemy. In much of his Gospel Luke tries to get us to see why Jesus was crucified—because his sermons and messages were often offensive to the good responsible Presbyerians, I mean Pharisees, of his day. The challenge is then ours. We hear it for ourselves dynamically. We in our day, like them n theirs, presume too much and assume too much of God. We aave perhaps domesticated God, made God a sort of guarantor of ur agendas, of what we know best. Prophetic critique is full of urprises of this sort (Isa. 28:21). It stresses that besides being he particular Redeemer of Israel, and the God present in Christ, God is the Creator of the whole world and of all peoples, and as uch is free to follow his own agenda.

Closely related to the technique of dynamic analogy in reading nd interpreting a text for today is the ancient principle from vhich it comes, that of "memory." In biblical terms the concept of emembering is the concept of recalling traditions about Israel's ast in such a way as to identify with those in the story who were ur ancestors in the faith. Judaism's annual reading of the com- lete Torah in the synagogue, parashah by parashah (paragraph) ach week, enables Jews to remember who they are. In the open- ng scene of *Fiddler on the Roof* Tevya sings of the function of radition in the life of a Jew: by reciting the traditions, especially he basic tradition, Torah, Jews are reminded—no matter where hey may be in the world, whether in times of crisis or when empted to assimilate to the dominant culture, in times of ease vhen identity so easily slips away—that they are Jews. The Torah tory reminds Jews constantly that they are the "people come out f Egypt" (Exod. 1:1); they are the slaves-freed-from-Egypt folk Exodus 12 and Joshua 24). Down through the centuries it has een the same. The Passover Haggadah stresses it. Memory hapes identity.

In effect, therefore, to remember God's mercies or deeds is to ecite the basic Torah story. It is to tell the story of what God as done and said: Creation, election, redemption from Egyptian lavery, guidance in the wilderness, suggestions as to how to shape ife and society at Sinai, entrance into the land. The remembrance f God's works tells the faithful who they are, even when the ontexts in which they live change, whether they live in or out of alestine, in this or that culture, under whatever threat, whether n pain or at ease.[23]

So also to remember Christ is to tell what for Christians is the climax of the Torah story, what God did in Christ according to the New Testament. To "do this in remembrance" of him, as Christ commanded the followers at the Last Supper, is to tell the story along with partaking of the bread and the cup. To do so means a sort of breaking down of the barriers of time and space. Just as the Jew experiences time transcended in remembering freedom from slavery and identifies with that first generation of redeemed slaves so that the ancient event is contemporized, so the Christian at the communion table experiences the presence of Christ and the disciples—and indeed of all the saints and martyrs of the church triumphant through the centuries. Not only is time transcended so that the church through the centuries once more knows who it is in the presence of "so great a cloud of witnesses" (Hebrews 12:1), but space is also transcended. The present church militant can experience the transcending of the walls of their meeting houses and cathedrals, and have a contemporary sense of the ecumenical nature of the living body of Christ now. Debates in church history about whether such re-presentation in the Eucharist was effected by transubstantiation (Catholic), "real" presence (Lutheran), or by an immediate act of the Holy Spirit dependent on the faith and intentionality of the participants (left-wing Reformation) all stem from this ancient concept.

In a context of worship and retelling the story remembrance is a powerful tradition, whether at Passover or in the Eucharist. To remember the work of God in Israel and in Christ is to have a renewed sense of who we are, no matter the context into which circumstances have moved us, no matter "where we are." Just as Jews refresh their self-knowledge of being liberated slaves (even in Miami Beach!) so Christians refresh their self-knowledge of being saved sinners (even in Claremont!).

And this may be done by reading the story not as though it were of events way back there about ancient folk but by reading it dynamically, identifying with those who provide us the best mirrors for our identity. The Bible, except in its Wisdom Literature and traditions, provides very few models of morality. An honest reading of the Bible indicates how many biblical characters were just as limited and full of shortcomings as we today. It would seem that about seventy-five percent of the Bible celebrates the theologem *errore hominum providentia divina:* God's providence works in and through human error and sin. The Bible offers no great or infallible models, no saints in the meaning that word has taken on since biblical times—nearly perfect people. None! It offers indeed very few models to follow at all except the work of God in Creation and in Israel in the Old Testament and the work of God in Christ in the New. Biblical people were just like us! Abraham and Sarah lied when they were scared (Gen. 12:13; 18:15) and laughed (Gen. 17:17; 18:12) when they could not believe their own ears or God either (see chapter 1 below). Jacob, our father, was a liar and supplanter (Gen. 27:19). Joseph was an obnoxious imp (Gen. 37:10). Moses was a murderer and fugitive from justice (Exod. 5:12–15).

The presentation of the disciples in all three synoptic Gospels follows the same theologem: they appear to be incredulous and even rather stupid. Judas's betrayal of Jesus is told in the same scenes as Peter's denial of Jesus and the bickering, sleep, and flight of all the disciples (Luke 22:3–62). When one has come to realize that God can take the selling of our brother Joseph into slavery and turn our evil into our later salvation (Gen. 50:20), then one has also realized that God has taken our selling of Christ to Caesar and made it our salvation. Then one also comes to thank God that Judas too was at the table at the Last Supper and that he also received the bread and the wine, because if he had not been there I could not now come to that table myself. God's greatest grace was manifest in the midst of the drama of betrayal. He gave us the broken bread on the very night we betrayed him (see chapter 6 below).

We need to read the Bible honestly, recognizing that much of it celebrates God's willingness to take our humanity, our frailty, and our limitations and weave them into his purposes. God's grace is not stumped by our limitations, indeed not even by Ramses' need of slave labor nor by Herod's fear of losing his position of power. Did Pharaoh's army pursue the fleeing slaves? Did Herod send troops to kill baby boys in Bethlehem? The answer to such questions lies not in "history," but in the theologem that God is not offended by either Pharaoh's chariots or Herod's swords. And that is reality. That meets us where we are in history, at whatever point of action, or of reaction to power shifting or threatening to shift from one base to another—and that is on every page of history. What could possibly thwart God's grace at this late date? What can a modern Ramses or Nebuchadnezzar or Herod or Pilate do, qualitatively, that could outreach such freedom or such grace?

Actually we should read the Bible with three Hs: honesty, humility, and humor. Honesty means recognition of the fact that much of the Bible celebrates God's grace working in and through human sin and weakness—the full human condition, which in the Bible is not made palatable to delicate sensibilities but is realistically portrayed. It also means that we cannot moralize while first reading most passages or sections of the Bible. To do that is to do what the ancient biblical writers refused to do—clean up the human condition in the Bible so as to make the individuals in it models for us to follow in our lives. Or if we read the Bible honestly and also moralize while doing so then we find ourselves thinking the absurd in supposing we should lie like Abraham and Jacob or kill like Moses in order for God to do his stuff with us. That is an abuse of the Bible. We have to theologize *first*, see what the passage indicates God is doing in and through the human condition portrayed, and only thereafter moralize or ask what the passage indicates we might do to shape our society and lives in the light of God's activity. We have first to look for God's works in the stories and then look for ours in the light of his. As Paul saw quite clearly after his conversion, we are "saved" by God's works, not by ours (Rom. 9:31–10:4).

Humility means identifying in the stories, reports, and parables with those with whom we might not otherwise identify: even the so-called bad guys in a story, for example with Joseph's brothers instead of with Joseph, or with the congregation at Nazareth instead of with Jesus (Luke 4:16–30) (see chapters 2 and 4 below).

Humor means taking God a little more seriously and ourselves a little less seriously day by day and on each reading. If we can't laugh at ourselves a little in the realism of life as the Bible portrays it we'll never get its message. We have to smile a bit when we see ourselves in Abraham fall prostrate before the deity in a posture of great piety and instead of praying see him (find ourselves) snickering at the thought that God can do the impossible (Gen. 18:14; Luke 1:37), especially without our help! There are many cases in the Bible where good humor about our frailties and disbeliefs is a necessity if we are to see ourselves in the mirrors the Bible affords. This is perhaps especially true in the grumbling of the faithful, a frequent biblical theme (see, e.g., Num. 11: 18–20 and Matt. 20:8–15).

Finally, the best way to understand the Bible as the churches' book today is to think of it primarily as a paradigm, not as a box or casket of gems and jewels to be mined. A paradigm is a pattern of function of a noun or verb in any language. The Bible comes to us from a twelve- to fifteen-hundred-year time span covering five different culture eras and reflecting the idioms and metaphors of all those cultures. But as a whole it should be viewed in large part as a paradigm in its function in the believing communities today. A paradigm, first, of the verbs and nouns of God's activities and speech, and then, thereupon, a putative paradigm of the verbs and nouns of our activities and speech, in our time and in our contexts. Just as verbs have finite forms and inflections, tenses, modes, and various functions, so the Bible as canon indicates the verbs of God's works, and hence ours in the light thereof. The ontology of the Bible as canon is that of paradigm addressing the faithful in context when they seriously ask the questions, who are we and what are we to do? The answers come in paradigms of faith (identity) and of obedience (lifestyle) appropriate to the contexts in which the questions seek them. There are a number of ways to recite the paradigm in our day and in our contexts—in liturgy, in drama, in dance, in sermons, and most of all by living thoughtfully in its reflection.

The God of the Bible is a God of grace and divine commitment in his promises and in his fulfillments; but he is also free to judge, challenge, and correct those to whom he is committed. The God of the Bible is a God of power, free to create and re-create as he wills; but he is also a God of great passion and suffering love. The God of the Bible is the God of all, the God of the universe; but he is one, not many, and his integrity must be affirmed despite the apparent fragmentation of all we see and witness. That to which his people are called to witness is the oneness of reality and its essential integrity. Genesis 1–11 attested to the integrity against an ancient backdrop of polytheism not much different from our own forms of polytheism and fragmented truth today.

Notes

1. While I have not been able to locate a published form of the Denver address, one can see Berger's main point in a lecture delivered a few years later titled "Religion in a Revolutionary Society" published in pamphlet by the American Enterprise Institute for Public Policy Research in Washington, D.C., 1974. See especially the statement on p. 16: "I am a Christian, which means that I have a stake in the churches' overcoming their 'failure of nerve' and regaining their authority in representing a message that I consider to be of ultimate importance for mankind."

2. Sam Keen, *To a Dancing God* (New York: Harper & Row Publishers, 1970); Harvey Cox, *The Seduction of the Spirit* (New York: Simon & Schuster, 1973); Malcolm Boyd, *Am I Running With You, God?* (Garden City: Doubleday & Co., 1977); Tom F. Driver, *Patterns of Grace: Human Experience as Word of God* (San Francisco: Harper & Row Publishers, 1977); William Sloane Coffin, Jr., *Once to Every Man: A Memoir* (New York: Atheneum Publishers, 1977).

3. See James A. Sanders, "Biblical Criticism and the Bible as Canon," *Union Seminary Quarterly Review* 32 (1977): 157–65.

4. Sanders, "Torah and Christ," *Interpretation* 29 (1975): 372–90.

5. George Mendenhall, *The Tenth Generation: The Origins of the Biblical Tradition* (Baltimore: Johns Hopkins Press, 1973).

6. James Barr, *The Bible in the Modern World* (New York: Harper & Row Publishers, 1973), p. 179, n. 11.

7. Ibid., pp. 130–31. An earlier response to Barr's book is in Sanders, "Reopening Old Questions about Scripture," *Interpretation* 28 (1974): 321–30.

8. There is considerable doubt that there was a so-called council of Jamnia. See Jack P. Lewis, "What Do We Mean by Jabneh?" *Journal of Bible and Religion* 32 (1964): 124–32; see also James A. Sanders, "Adaptable for Life: The Nature and Function of Canon," *Magnalia Dei: The Mighty Acts of God*, ed. Frank M. Cross, Werner E. Lemke, and P. D. Miller (Garden City: Doubleday & Co., 1976), pp. 531–36.

9. See E. W. Nicholson, *Preaching to the Exiles* (New York: Schocken Books, 1971), pp. 93–103; H. Weippert, *Die Prosareden des Jeremiahbuches*, Beihefte zur Zeitschrift für die alttestamentliche Wissenschaft 132 (Berlin: Walter de Gruyter, 1973); and W. Holladay, "A Fresh Look at 'Source B' and 'Source C' in Jeremiah," *Vetus Testamentum* 25 (1975): 394–412.

10. See Sanders, "Adaptable for Life," pp. 537ff.

11. Barr, *Old and New in Interpretation* (New York: Harper & Row Publishers, 1966), p. 27.

12. For a more systematic treatment of what follows see Sanders, "Hermeneutics," *Interpreter's Dictionary of the Bible Supplement* (New York: Abingdon Press, 1976), pp. 402–7.

13. See William Shires, *Finding the Old Testament in the New* (Philadelphia: Westminster Press, 1974), pp. 13–77; Daniel Patte, *Early Jewish Hermeneutic in Palestine* (Missoula, Mont.: Scholars Press, 1975); and Richard Longenecker, *Biblical Exegesis in the Apostolic Period* (Grand Rapids: Wm. B. Eerdmans Publishing Co., 1975).

14. For a list with short descriptions of some of the current reactions to biblical criticism see Sanders, "Biblical Criticism and the Bible as Canon."

15. See, among others, Patte, *What Is Structural Exegesis?* (Philadelphia: Fortress Press, 1976).

16. For instance Micah (3:12) was cited almost "accurately" at Jeremiah's first trial (Jer. 26:18) with conscious effort to reconstruct the reaction of the government in Micah's time to what he had said. Even so, the focus in the trial was on the relevance of Micah's case to Jeremiah's.

17. For a vigorous statement to this effect see B. J. Roberts, "Bible Exegesis and Fulfillment in Qumran," *Words and Meanings,* ed. Peter R. Ackroyd and Barnabas Lindars (Cambridge: Cambridge University Press, 1968); see also Sanders, "From Isaiah 61 to Luke 4," *Christianity, Judaism and Other Greco-Roman Cults,* ed. J. Neusner, part 1 (Leiden: Brill, 1975), pp. 75–106.

18. For a vigorous (perhaps exaggerated) statement on this point see Walter Wink, *The Bible and Human Transformation: Toward a New Paradigm of Biblical Study* (Philadelphia: Fortress Press, 1973).

19. See Sanders, "Habakkuk in Qumran, Paul, and the Old Testament," *Journal of Religion* 38 (1959): 232–44; Geza Vermes, *Scripture and Tradition* (Leiden: Brill, 1973); Brevard Childs, *Biblical Theology in Crisis* (Philadelphia: Westminster Press, 1970); and Sanders, "The Canon of Scripture," *Oral and Literary Tradition in Judaism and Early Christianity,* ed. Roger Le Déaut, Vermes et al. (Amsterdam: van Gorcum, 1979).

20. See Sanders, "Hermeneutics," especially the bibliography; see also the appendixes to idem, *Identité de la Bible* (Paris: Cerf, 1975), pp. 153–67.

21. Sanders, "Hermeneutics of True and False Prophecy," *Canon and Authority,* ed. George W. Coats and Burke O. Long (Philadelphia: Fortress Press, 1977), pp. 21–41.

22. See, for instance, Gerhard Von Rad, *Wisdom in Israel,* tr. James D. Martin (New York: Abingdon Press, 1973).

23. Sanders, "Torah and Christ."

PART ONE

THE FREEDOM OF THE
GOD OF GRACE

1. Promise and Providence

"Promise and Providence" was written in the spring of 1965 and preached in The Brick Church, Presbyterian, at Rochester, New York, on 23 May 1965. The occasion was valedictory. Mrs. Sanders and I had decided the previous December that I should accept the invitation from Union Theological Seminary to move to New York City and take up residence there as professor of Old Testament. We loved Brick Church and had been active participants in its life for some ten years. Dr. David A. MacLennan, our pastor, was at General Assembly in Columbus, Ohio. I had preached at Brick occasionally before and often taught the adult forum class on Sunday mornings, so the congregation was already acquainted with some of the basic hermeneutic rules I espoused, especially that of reading some biblical stories as mirrors for our own identity as the elect or church of God today. Some of them remembered "Banquet of the Dispossessed" (see chapter 5 below) which I had preached at Brick the previous August just after the searing riots and looting in Rochester's hot summer of 1964.

Brick Church had supported the Presbytery of Rochester (now Genesee Valley) in its sponsorship—through the Council of Churches —of Saul Alinsky, the community organizer from Chicago, who came to Rochester after the 1964 riots. That support caused dissension and the nine intervening months had not been easy for the church or the city. We had come to realize how sinful we as God's people really are. I felt I had two messages to deliver that morning, each closely woven with the other. Rochester's great self-regard had been severely damaged. The designation Smugtown USA had been deserved at least in part, and that because of how intensely the city was loved by its prominent citizens, not a few of whom belonged to Brick Church. After all, it was the city of Walter Rauschenbusch; many felt that it already practiced the social gospel and did not deserve either the riots or Saul Alinsky. For those who deeply felt that Rochester did not *merit* the indictments being hurled at it by its poor I wanted so to open the Bible that we would be reminded that neither had we *merited* God's grace nor indeed much of which we had been proud.

Then too I thought that we all needed reminding of the very nature of *church* and the essential meaning of election.

A decontextualized form of the sermon with a few footnotes to comfort scholars was published in the *Union Seminary Quarterly Review* (hereafter cited as *USQR*) 21 (1966): 295–303. There it is stated that the sermon was delivered in James Chapel at Union Seminary on Sunday, 30 January 1966; that is true, and I have preached it many times since, sometimes by specific request. It has been adaptable to more than one context, but the above was the original context, and the following the original text.

Jesus says in our morning Gospel lesson from Luke 24:49, "And behold, I send the promise of my Father upon you; but stay in the city, until you are clothed with power from on high." Thereafter is recorded the experience of the Ascension from Bethany, which Christians the world over will celebrate this week, on Thursday, in the Christian calendar. Luke quite frequently identified the Spirit with the power of God—and quite rightly so both from the standpoint of Old Testament usage and from the vantage point of semitic philology. *Ruaḥ*, or "spirit" in Hebrew, primarily means sheer force or power, precisely and well pictured by Luke at Pentecost both as a rushing wind and as flames of fire.

Professor Bo Reicke of the University of Basel has recently written, "Luke's predominant interest is quite evidently the continuity, in the drama of redemption, between the old and new covenants. . . . Early Christianity," he continued, "loved the Old Testament, and those who transmitted the gospel of the kingdom were interested in the history of election."[*]

If one asks the most basic, elementary questions about the history of election and the nature of the church, that is, of the Israel of God—how it came into being, how it is sustained, in what its life obtains, on what its existence depends—he is in effect asking the very questions to which the book of Genesis is addressed. When one speaks of Israel, that is, the church or people of God, he is speaking of the community of the elect, of those, as Peter

---

[*]Bo Reicke, *The Gospel of Luke* (Richmond: John Knox Press, 1964), pp. 58–59.

says in his Pentecost sermon in Acts, "whom the Lord our God calls to him." The definition of the church, *qahal* in Hebrew, *ekklēsia* in Greek, is "the community of those called by God: his elect people." And if we go to the Gospel of Luke and to the Acts of the Apostles with the primary question of what church or election is all about, Luke himself in both books refers us directly to the history of election which is the Old Testament. Indeed it is assumed that we would already know all about election, how God chose for himself a people to love and to bless whose mission and task it is to be an instrument of blessing for the whole world, for the whole of creation. For the church should annually read the whole biblical story in its various parts from Genesis through the gospel, and thus identify with its origins.

And Genesis puts it clearly and simply. God is the elector and Israel, in the patriarchs, is the elected. Sometimes we Presbyterians get a little confused on this matter and think that in our annual general assembly, which is meeting this week in Columbus, it is we who elect God each year. No, the elector is God, clearly stated in Genesis as the Creator of the whole world, of all that is, one God of all. God is the life giver and sustainer. It is he who has life to give and to bestow. Life, being, existence depend utterly on him. Man does not have life except that God gives it to him. It is not a possession of man; it is a gift of God.

And in answering the other elementary question of who is the elected, or whom did God elect, Genesis is equally clear: Out of the morass of confusion of people of all the earth's races and tongues God chose one man. (As a student once wrote in a term paper, "He always starts with one man.") And God said to Abraham, Go to the place which I shall show you and I will bless you so that you may be a blessing to all the families of the earth.

And to that man he made a promise which would be to his children for generations to come: I will make of you a great nation, and I will bless you, and make your name great, so that you will be a blessing.

From that point on Genesis addresses itself to the ultimate question of faith: Can or will God keep his promise? The promise is that from Abraham would issue the people of God. But we are told already in Genesis 11:30 that he is childless and that

Sarai, his wife, is barren—and the line must come through the matriarch. Will she and Abraham have a child? Genesis chapters 12 through 21 have as their one overarching, all-consuming interest the question, Will Sarai bear Abraham a son? Will there even be a start made on fulfilling the promise? Or will the whole proposition founder on Sarai's barrenness?

One of the first problems dealt with in the story is whether Abraham merited this election. How was he chosen? Why Abraham? Why not someone else? Was Abraham such a paragon of righteousness that he deserved this election? Let us journey with them and see. They set out from their home in Haran and settled in Palestine. Soon there was a famine in the land and, as often in the Bible, they had to go down to Egypt where food was abundant. So Abraham and Sarai set out. Now Sarai was a beautiful woman and Abraham, fearing for his life, said to Sarai: Since you are so beautiful, when the Egyptians see you they will want you for themselves, and if they know that I am your husband they will kill me in order to get you. Therefore tell them you are my sister "that it may go well with me because of you, and that my life may be spared on your account."

Had God chosen Abraham because he was truthful, honest, brave, and dependable? For right away we are told that Abraham lied in order to save his life. How much do you think he believed in God's promise? How much stock do you think he put by God's providence? Manifestly no more than we do.

No, I fear that we are disabused immediately of the delusion that Abraham was chosen because of his faith or because of his belief. And if that were not enough we are told in the following verses that Abraham was paid well when Pharaoh took Sarai into his harem. Far from being a paragon of virtue our father Abraham now appears in quite another light. And this is the point we must never lose sight of. Each year as we read this account of our election in Abraham as God's people, we see ourselves well reflected. Do we deserve this election? Do we merit God's choosing us, the church, as his people, the vessel he has chosen by which to bless the world? The answer given from Genesis to Revelation in the Bible is a resounding no. We do not merit God's love and grace; we do not deserve this election. For here we stand before

Pharaoh selling our wife Sarai into his harem. In the Bible election means only humility—never pride. To say we are the elect of God is not to brag or boast, it is to confess *our* sins and *God's* grace.

Every year we must read this story. Every year we the elect church of God must see ourselves afresh, in our father Abraham, sell our beloved Sarai to Pharaoh. And here is the point: we in all our finery and high self-regard must confess that we are not one whit better than our father Abraham. Until we, each of us, can confess that we sold her to Pharaoh, until we, each of us, can confess that we sold Christ to Caesar—out of fear for ourselves, out of fear for our lives, out of fear for existence—we cannot go on to confess God's grace and forgiveness.

What does it mean to be the elect of God? It means first and foremost abject humility. "And for Sarai's sake Pharaoh dealt well with Abram; and he had sheep, oxen, he-asses, menservants, maidservants, she-asses, and camels." But he did not have Sarai. He had sold her to Pharaoh. Abram, like ourselves, feared Pharaoh's power more than he believed in God's providence. Where now is God's promise? Abraham is rich, but Sarai our mother is another man's wife. Has the whole story foundered at the outset?

And then we must read the next paragraph which says, "The Lord afflicted Pharaoh and his house with great plagues because of Sarai, Abram's wife." Pharaoh, who hadn't done anything wrong according to his best lights, who honestly thought Sarai was only Abraham's sister and therefore eligible for his harem, must submit to the power of God for Abraham's sake. Pharaoh gets the divine message through his afflictions and calls Abraham in and asks what it is he has done to him. And then we must, annually, endure perhaps the most humiliating experience of all. For here Pharaoh lectures our father Abraham on ethics:

> Why did you not tell me that she was your wife? Why did you say, "She is my sister," so that I took her for my wife? Now then, here is your wife, take her, and be gone.

"And Pharaoh gave men orders concerning him; and they set him on the way, with his wife and all that he had." Not only is it the nonelect Pharaoh who seems more virtuous than Abraham, it is Pharaoh who first lectures us, in Abraham, on ethics.

Thus closes the first chapter of the story of our election. And the sum of it is devastating. Our humility is established. Our lack of real faith in God and belief in his power is confirmed. We have narrowly escaped losing Sarai and the means to the fulfillment of the promise. If it had not been for God's power and Pharaoh's ethics there would be no mother and no human hope for the great elect people of the promise.

But even so there is still no child. Sarai remains barren. In chapter after chapter we must read of one narrow escape after the other, with the primary question ever uppermost in our minds: Will there be an heir to the promise? Will a child be born to this union? First there is the battle reported between Abraham with his meagre force of 318 men against the overwhelming odds of the combined armies of the city-state kings of Canaan. What if he loses? The very existence of the church hangs in the balance. Abraham won, but still Sarai has no child. Following the Bronze Age customs of the time Sarai commends to Abraham her maid-servant, the Egyptian Hagar. And Hagar bears for Abraham the Arab Ishmael, who according to the laws and customs of the times might have become the heir of Abraham and hence the recipient of the promise. In other words the Arabs might have received the promise instead of Israel. And according to the Bronze Age Hittite laws only recently recovered we now know that if Abraham had had no son, no heir of his own blood, his heritage would have fallen on his major domo, his chief steward Eliezer of Damascus. That is to say each year we must be reminded that a Syrian might have received the blessing and hence the promise: the Syrians might have been the church, the people of God, instead of Israel.

Then finally God told Abraham that Sarah would bear him a son. "Then Abraham fell on his face and laughed, and said to himself, 'Shall a child be born to a man who is a hundred years old? Shall Sarah, who is ninety years old, bear a child?'" And then as though to scare us to death Abraham pleads with God for a little sanity in the situation, something reasonable, and says,

"O that Ishmael might live in thy sight!" Our father Abraham, because he cannot believe that God could bless Sarah with a son in their old age, begs that Ishmael, the Arab, be accepted of God for his special people. What a mockery of Abraham's exalted belief in God's promise! When in chapter 15 God told Abraham that his descendants would be as numerous as the stars in heaven Abraham looked up, was impressed, and the text says, "he believed the Lord; and he reckoned it to him as righteousness." I suppose when we look up at the stars we think we believe. But what about when all human means of fulfillment of the promise have been exhausted? What about when we've reached a hundred years old and the promise is still unfulfilled? We laugh at the prospect of God's managing to fulfill his promise without our help. How can we have a child, we are too old. It's ridiculous. Won't Ishmael do? Abraham loved his son, the Arab Ishmael. Thank God for that. But real faith and real belief he has not. I think we see ourselves well reflected in our father Abraham.

And then when God, in the three visitors, in chapter 18 also told Sarah that she would bear a son, she too laughed out of her unbelief, her lack of faith that God could keep a promise. And so God said that the child's name would be *Yiẓḥaq*, Isaac, meaning "he laughs." Isaac's very name would stand forever as a reminder of our unbelief, of our laughing at God.

And then there are the episodes in chapters 19 to 21 which threaten even yet the arrival of the heir, the birth of the son. There is the destruction of Sodom, the journey to Gerar and Sarah's joining another harem through Abraham's disbelief, and the second episode in chapter 21 with Hagar and Ishmael even after Isaac is born.

But finally, nay annually, we must read in chapter 22 those earth-shattering words of God to Abraham, "Take your son, your only begotten son Isaac, whom you love, and go to the land of Moriah, and offer him there as a burnt offering upon one of the mountains of which I shall tell you." Isaac is born. The heir has come. The son born to Sarah after her menopause, after it was humanly impossible for her to have a son, the son born as an unmistakable gift of God, the son of Abraham's extreme maturity, the apple of his eye, God commands him to sacrifice, to give up, to surrender. God had given Isaac. God had kept his promise. The boy had come and life once more had meaning. There was hope. There would be a people of God. The lineage was secured. All was well. Abraham had Isaac and nothing else mattered. And then he heard those shattering words, "Take your son . . . whom you love . . . and offer him . . ."

Never forget that Isaac was the two things to Abraham: his beloved and only son, and the gift of God—the link to the progeny, the people of God which was to issue from him. Abraham loved this gift, this blessing, as only a mature father knows how. Abraham poured his life into that boy. Abraham counted on him completely as his heir. The whole future of the promise, the whole proposition of the people-of-God idea depended on Isaac: he was the single link. The whole church, the whole future people in that sense resided in Isaac. As it is so clearly stated in the Hebrew of Genesis 21:12, "For in Isaac is your progeny called." In Isaac resided all the future generations of the church. Without him there would be no church. In him we lived or did not live; in him we existed or did not exist. On him the whole proposition of the called people of God depended. We are in Isaac. The history of the election hangs in the balance and we hear, must hear annually, those shocking words, "Take your son . . . and offer him . . ."

First let us dispense with the utter nonsense of asking how a good God can ask such a think of Abraham. To ask that question is never to have understood anything whatever about election. To ask that question is to be ignorant of the Bible and of the biblical God. To ask that question is to escape reality. For reality forces us to realize that the church, the promise, the election, the people do not ultimately depend on Isaac any more at this point than they depended on Sarah's ability or inability to have children. The existence of the church, our being, our existence depend utterly, completely, and totally on God. But in Abraham we can see our own human tendency to believe that existence depends on God's gifts rather than on God the giver of those gifts. And this passage says to us that whenever we are seduced, as indeed we constantly are, to think that our existence depends on creation or that the church depends on the church, we must face the divine question, the judgment of God on our very life: Have we mistaken God's gift for God the giver? Have we come to think that the guarantee of existence resides in ourselves? Then God must, though it break his heart, God must, in his infinite goodness, make his beloved friend Abraham face up to the ultimate question of where his commitment lies.

Abraham loved Isaac, as well he should. That is not the point. Of course we love God's gifts. Of course we enjoy God's gifts. But in so doing we are daily, constantly under the temptation to believe that the gifts have an independent existence of their own, that they somehow contain their own existence and guarantee their own being. We daily want to believe that the gift is its own giver—and that is naught other than what the Bible simply calls sin. Abraham was right to love Isaac with all his heart and with all his being. But he was wrong if he thought the future depended on Isaac's life. He was wrong if he thought the promise of God depended on the boy. What if, as when Israel lost its independence and its very existence as a state in the Babylonian exile, what if Isaac were taken away? What if Christ was crucified and laid in the tomb? Would all then be lost? Would we not have to face up to our basic unbelief?

"Offer him as burnt offering." Do you really believe in the promise and providence of God? Does the promise depend on Isaac or on God, on the gift or the Giver? "So Abraham rose early in the morning . . . and took two of his young men with him, and his son Isaac; and he cut the wood for the burnt offering, and arose and went to the place of which God had told him. . . . And Abraham took the wood of the burnt offering and laid it on Isaac his son; and he took in his hand the fire and the knife. So they went both of them together." You cannot read this story with your feet on your desk. You know the outcome for you've read it every year all your life long. But each time you hear it you learn again the meaning of love and the meaning of sin. But you must each time accompany Abraham on this journey. For you know you are Abraham and you know that the question of existence has fallen on you. Where does the guarantee lie? In the gift or in the Giver? Where does providence lie? In ourselves or in God? That is the question here in Genesis 22, and that is the question of the cross—which can never be erased.

You know very well the outcome of the story. You know that Abraham and Isaac climbed the mountain together. You remember how Abraham built the stone altar with his own hands and then bound his son upon the wood on the altar. And you remember in your heart of hearts the scene thus described, "Then Abraham put forth his hand, and took the knife to slay his son." And you know that you can never escape it, for you know that in the reality of that scene resides the question of existence. If that knife falls, the one link in the continuity of the church has perished at the hand of the elect Abraham himself. That is the moment of truth for the church, the whole future and idea of which resides in Isaac on that altar. For unless we truly believe that God, being God, has the right to ask that question which that knife poses poised in midair, then we cannot go on in faith to hear those next joyous words which filled the whole air as by a chorus of angels, "Abraham, do not lay your hand on the lad or do anything to him; for now I know that you fear God (and not his gifts), seeing you have not withheld your son, your only son, from me."

Thus did the God who once gave Isaac give him yet a second time. Thus did the God who first placed Isaac in Sarah's barren womb replace him in his father's arms. Thus did the God who first gave life to Isaac give life to him again. Thus do we know of a certainty that it is God who gives, it is God on whom existence depends. As St. Paul said, it is in him that we live and move and have our being. The fallacy of thinking that life exists independently of God is inherent in us all, for sin is essentially our failure to distinguish the Giver and the gift. And we must all collectively in some sense know the judgment upon us of the commandment which tears at the heart of God himself, "Take your son, your only begotten son . . ." For we cannot forget that this is the same God who later, we are told, will have the same experience.

But we all know the end of the story, how the ram caught in the thicket by his horns became the substitute offering. "So Abraham called the name of that place The Lord will provide; as it is said

to this day, 'On the mount of the Lord it shall be provided.' "
For God's providence is precisely his commitment to fulfill his
promise of a church. It is the power of God, his Holy Spirit, to
keep his promise. But it is also a beneficent reminder that he
alone is God. He who gives life the first time can also give it
again. The marvel in the Bible is not Resurrection or re-Creation
but Creation. For belief in the first is already belief in the
second.

Then Jesus said to them, "Everything written about me in the
law of Moses and the prophets and the psalms must be fulfilled.
. . . Thus it is written, that the Christ should suffer and on the
third day rise from the dead. . . . You are witnesses of these
things. And behold, I send the promise of my Father upon you
. . ." As Paul so clearly declared to the church in Galatia, "There
is neither Jew nor Greek, there is neither slave nor free, there is
neither male nor female; for you are all one in Christ Jesus. And
if you are Christ's, then you are Abraham's offspring, heirs according to the promise."

○   ○   ○

For the benediction I shall use the closing remarks of Paul's
second letter to the church at Corinth:

Examine yourselves, to see whether you are holding to your faith.
Test yourselves. Do you not realize that Jesus Christ is in you?—
unless indeed you fail to meet the test! I hope you will find out
that we have not failed. But we pray God that you may not do
wrong—not that we may appear to have met the test, but that
you may do what is right, though we may seem to have failed.
For we cannot do anything against the truth, but only for the
truth. For we are glad when we are weak and you are strong.
What we pray for is your improvement . . .

Finally, brethren, farewell. Mend your ways, heed the appeal,
agree with one another, live in peace, and the God of love and
peace will be with you. Greet one another with a holy kiss. All the
saints greet you.

And the grace of the Lord Jesus Christ and the love of God
and the fellowship of the Holy Spirit be with you all. Amen.

2. The New History: Joseph Our Brother

"Joseph Our Brother" grew in two stages. The first part was written for a summer session chapel service at Union Seminary in July 1967. The second part specifically on Joseph, beginning with "Let us look closely now at a biblical story . . ." (p. 47), was written for delivery along with the first part at the annual luncheon sponsored by the Ministers and Missionaries Benefit Board of the American Baptist Convention meeting in Boston on 29 May 1968. It was published as a pamphlet by the board but is no longer available as such.

I had for some years been trying to understand our Lord's commandment to love the enemy. I still am not sure I understand it, but I do know that I am not satisfied with the individualistic and paternalizing interpretation we hear so often—that it means we should love the doer but not the deed if the latter is viewed as somehow evil or wrong. For example, we do not have to love the mugging to love the mugger. But I wonder: do we love the mugger in such a case or have we but found a way to go down feeling superior? This poor mugger is really the victim of society or the system—not I. On the other hand does the commandment call on us to be a doormat for every bully on the block? How can you fight your battles if you love the enemy? Does this commandment cancel out all those others in the Bible which clearly call on the faithful to fight evil?

The commandment was issued by our Lord in a highly eschatological context in which the end of history was soon expected, and the ethic propounded for that penultimate time is surely not to be generalized into a universal principle. Right. But how can we understand it? Pluralistically. As a summons to be monotheistic pluralists. God is the God of all sides of our contextual conflicts. We have to fight evil as we understand evil in the light of value systems deriving from our particular(istic) story of redemption; but we have to keep that in tension with value systems deriving from our other belief that there is but one God of all creation, of all of us, including our occasional enemies.

41

So far so good. Then I read of the work of Robert Lively, at that time at Princeton, and his idea of "the new history." It seemed worth exploring and comparing. Later, while in Princeton for other purposes, I visited with Lively and discussed some implications.

Then in the fall of 1967 Howard Moody and others responsible for the Ministers and Missionaries Board luncheon in Boston the next May asked me to speak on the occasion. How much can happen in one year's time? Union experienced its first student revolt in 1967 and this was followed the next spring by the famous Columbia Bust. Classes were suspended and Union went into a "free university" session; governance was totally revamped. Nearly everybody in sight became singularists. Feelings became facts, we were told. And it was happening all over the world.

And in the midst of all that, not long after the actual bust at Columbia, on the Friday just before Palm Sunday Martin Luther King, Jr. was assassinated in Memphis.

On the day that I flew up to Boston to deliver the luncheon address, the Northeast was under torrential rains. I could not reach the shuttle plane I had planned to catch out of La Guardia; Grand Central Parkway in Queens was impassable. I caught the last possible shuttle out of Newark and arrived in the packed banquet hall soaked. A friend grabbed a cup of black coffee, stuck it in my hand, and escorted me to the rostrum where the first thing I did was take off my shoes. I delivered the address in wet stocking feet.

But more important than my discomfort was my ignorance of the immediate context. Apparently the black caucus of the convention had kept the delegates up the night before with their protests and demands. But no one had the time to tell me. I just knew it was May 1968. Apparently for the first time ever, the blacks of the convention segregated themselves for lunch at three tables near the rostrum. They were tense and so was the rest of the convention, some two thousand people in the hall. Beginning about halfway through the speech the blacks began to celebrate what they heard, punctuating and accenting as they listened. Mystified, but led as I think by the Spirit, I plowed on through the manuscript in my wet stocking feet, sniffling as little as possible. By the end of the speech there was such noise as northern Baptists of any color are not wont to make.

While speaking I was not fully aware of the immediate context into which I spoke, only of the general turmoil of the day. Those who dare may speak of the conjunction of the following text and that

Boston context as coincidence. But there are other words for it as well.

Genesis 37:1–11
Matthew 5:43–48

A press notice in the *New York Times* of 23 July 1967 carried the report that scholars at Princeton's Secondary School History Institute are, in the words of the report, "attempting to bring the study of history in high school to the level of sophistication of the 'new math.'" According to the institute director, Professor Robert A. Lively, "Students across the country, who are breathtakingly sophisticated in the 'new math' and new sciences, are learning history from bland, pallid textbooks which actually conflict with what they have observed and experienced. Their classes consist of meaningless notetaking and irrelevant monologues by teachers who may themselves be tied to textbooks simply because they haven't read anything else." The new approach being developed at the Princeton institute is called the "new history." New history exposes the student to controversy and more than one side of issues, and attempts to guide him to reach conclusions for himself rather than presenting him with a complete or closed interpretation. Like the new math and the new physics it emphasizes ways of thinking rather than facts.

It would be difficult for me to exaggerate the importance I attach to this report and to the efforts it describes. I should like to advance a theological thesis and then attempt to demonstrate and clarify the thesis insofar as time allows. Thesis: where the church through the centuries has failed to convince the world that God is the Lord of history, secular education in the methodology of the new history may succeed.

I have for some time been trying to understand the logion in Matthew to the effect that love of the enemy qualifies us as sons of our Father who is in heaven, who himself sends the blessings of sun and rain on both the just and the unjust, the good and the evil. This logion appears to me to have far more depth than any commentary or scholarly literature treating it—and there is no lack of such literature. What the logion potentially says is that we qualify to be sons of God—that is, become like members of the heavenly council or court, capable of surveying the whole of the human experiment from above it, or at least from outside it— at that point when we come fully to realize, no matter how difficult it may be, that God, our God, *our* heavenly Father is God of the other side also. Jesus says we qualify to be sons of God at that point when like God we too love both sides of our conflicts, when, in theological terms, we have become monotheistic pluralists. The end of the passage in Matthew 5 goes on to say that we must be like God precisely in that we must love those who do not love us, just as he loves those who do not appear to us to love him. In God such a quality is called absolute grace. And Jesus says that we must strive to be perfect like God so that like him we may come to love both sides of our conflicts. One observation very clear to the new historian, or to any good historian, is that terms such as good and bad, just and unjust are used by both sides in all conflicts: good and just always apply to the in-group and bad and unjust apply to the out-group. ("Bonnie and Clyde" have helped us humanize "The Untouchables.") The biblically oriented Christian, I must say at this point, does not abandon his use of the words good, bad, just, and unjust because they of necessity appear to the historian to be relative: To obey the commandment to love one's enemy does not mean that one abandons all the other commandments which presuppose ethical standards. To obey the commandment to love one's enemy does mean however that even the most ethically oriented Christian must affirm that God, the Lord of history, alone is the final Judge and Redeemer of all man's striving, including his obedience to ethical principles and his crusades for good.

This commandment to love our enemies is the judgment of God which truly lies athwart all views of good guys and bad guys. It is the one commandment which if heeded and obeyed brings into the present the historical perspective we shall surely have in the future on our current situation; it is the commandment which makes available to us, no matter how dimly, God's lordship over history. Loving our enemy today means listening to *his* hopes and fears: it means learning what is right about what is wrong and what is wrong about what is right. Loving our enemy, I suggest, is for today precisely the means of listening to the voice of God in this age of the death or silence of God.

Frankly I am thrilled to think that my twelve-year-old son, who is in the seventh grade, may be required now to read of the battle of New Orleans not only from the American point of view but also from the British point of view. One of the advantages of living near the Niagara frontier, as we did for eleven years, is that you know there were only good guys on both sides of the War of 1812. That observation is rather safe, I suppose. It usually takes about a century for us to love our enemies. I suppose most of us are finally prepared to admit that there were only good guys in both the blue and gray in our own Civil War. (And this is quite a concession for one born and bred to be a "southern gentleman"!) But Jesus' commandment and the new history would require us to view our present conflicts as though we lived a hundred years from now. It is still a bit dizzying for my generation to realize that the Japanese and Germans also had their hopes and fears just as we did. If God is truly God of us all and if the new history takes hold in our schools, it may become increasingly impossible for any people to view another people as totally evil and bad, as you and I tended to view the Germans and Japanese. Could it be that like Lincoln and Grant all Ho Chi Minh and Pham Van Dong really want to do is preserve the union of North and South Vietnam despite American efforts to retain power in Southeast Asia, like France's final effort in the 1860s to retain power in North America by aiding the Southern Confederacy?

Exodus 15 is called the anthem at the close of ancient Israel's annual cultic celebration of the Exodus. It starts, "I will sing to the Lord, for he has triumphed gloriously; the horse and his rider he has thrown into the sea . . ." It continues, "Pharaoh's chariots and his host he cast into the sea; and his picked officers are sunk in the Reed Sea." We must assume that this new history is going to cause students to want to go research the Egyptian point of view on that event. Is there no modern analogy to Pharaoh's position? What was his point of view when he told these ancient abolitionists, emancipators, and freedom-movement leaders, "Hold on now, you're moving too fast"? Was Pharaoh a bad guy, or does he provide a mirror for a people whose annual budget is $80 billion to kill people but far less for all forms of aid to the poor?

What will our children who study this new history do with Judas Iscariot? Judas Iscariot we assume was a bad guy. The New Testament in its very dangerous flirtation with dualism says that Satan entered into him—thereby making him forever unavailable to us for understanding, sympathy, or identification. Is one possessed of the devil because he opposes European colonialism in Palestine—as Judas opposed Roman imperialism in his own beloved country? Can one not understand a patriot who would finally become disillusioned with a teacher who when the chips were down said, "Render unto Caesar what is Caesar's"? Was Judas a bad guy to follow the advice of his church leaders Annas and Caiaphas that this messianic pretender might prematurely bring down the Roman legions and crush all hope of successful liberation? Was Judas a bad guy to receive of the church an honorarium for services rendered? For whom, our children pursuing the new history will ask of their parent generation, for whom is Judas not available as a mirror for self-understanding? And the Romans? The Romans after all were simply trying to wage the peace and maintain the Pax Romana even in a small out-of-the-way country. Are the Romans not available as a mirror for self-understanding?

This business of loving the enemy, that is, understanding the hopes and fears on both sides of human conflicts, may now with the new history begin to capture men's minds, not in the church which has always romantically interpreted the commandment individualistically to mean one should love the doer but not the deed, but rather in secular education where the new history, which will never mention God, may offer precisely that perspective which can affirm that God is the Lord of history, even he who sends the sun on the good and the bad and the rain on the just and the unjust. And the new history may even bring us to the shocking realization of what we should have seen all along: Moses, our liberator, prophet-mediator, and lawgiver, was a murderer and a fugitive from Egyptian justice; and Christ our Lord and Savior was accused of being a *lēstēs*, a man accused, tried, and executed for rebellion and sedition against Rome. Ancient Egypt and ancient Rome provide the mirrors necessary for us to see that Moses and Jesus from the official American viewpoint would have been bad guys. But the Bible says that it was through the one and in the other that God revealed justice and salvation to the world.

This new history may be a very interesting venture. By such a methodology our children may actually learn to read the Bible as the radical book of judgment of all sides that it is rather than as the support for "our" side which every side has misread it to be. "You have heard it was said, 'You shall love your neighbor and hate your enemy.' But I say to you, love your enemies . . . so that you may be sons of your Father who is in heaven."

Let us look closely now at a biblical story which I daresay is one of the favorites of all of us here. But let us hear the story in a way a bit different from the way we normally hear it. Let us in hearing it this time try to obey Jesus' command and try to new-history it by seeing the other side.

Joseph was Jacob's eleventh son and, like Isaac to Abraham, the child of his old age; but unlike the only begotten Isaac, Joseph was one of twelve sons. Joseph was his father's favorite and most beloved. Jealous brothers can tolerate paternal favoritism for a young child, but Joseph at the beginning of our story was seventeen years old when his father fitted him out in a fashion of haute couture beyond anything the brothers had had. Because of such favoritism in an elderly parent for the youngest and not the eldest son, the brothers' jealousy increased into petty behavior. The text says, "They hated him and could not speak peaceably to him." The Hebrew indicates they wouldn't even greet him a daily "Shalom." Or in our idiom, they wouldn't give him the time of day.

It is at this point that our usual reading of the Joseph story goes astray, for it is here that we begin to identify with Joseph in reading the story and thus miss the whole message. To identify even unconsciously with Joseph here is comparable to identifying with Christ at the later stage of the biblical story. Our superego hardly permits us to make common cause with hate, and our own plight as portrayed by the brothers becomes the undesirable characteristic of the bad guys which we assume any decent story should have. The job of translating a biblical text is at best a difficult one, and the hardest task is finding the right analogy so as to bring out the offensive judgment of God which alone saves and redeems. If I dared to submit a new hermeneutic rule for biblical interpretation it would be this: whenever our reading of a biblical passage makes us feel self-righteous we can be sure that we have misread it; and the concomitant rule would be: whenever our reading of a biblical passage brings home to us the poignant judgment and salvation of God's humility we can be confident we have read it correctly. Hermeneutics is, as Professor James Robinson suggests, the means whereby a translator or interpreter scores the same point today that the original author or speaker intended. I am confident that original biblical points can never be scored until it is recognized (*a*) that in reading any story or historical account we commonly seek out the most compatible force or character in it, that is, we being by nature dualists and polytheists immediately divide up sides into good guys and bad guys; and (*b*) that we then, even if unconsciously, identify with the good guys. Some such process is what normally happens when we read the gospel so that we mistakenly identify with Christ and get angry at Judas, Pilate, Annas and Caiaphas, and the rest, rather than identifying with the latter so that we can then hear the word of forgiveness and know the judgment of God which alone saves and redeems. It is also what we normally do in reading the Joseph story, and I want right here at the start, already at Gen. 37:4, to steer you into the much more difficult psychological path of identifying with the church, that is, with Jacob and the eleven sons.

The writer of the story, who was without question a genius, goes on to attempt to get us to do just that. As Thomas Mann in his novel *Joseph and His Brothers* saw quite clearly, the writer portrays the young Joseph as an imp. Joseph not only claims his father's favor, he goes on to attempt to claim divine favor. Joseph had two dreams, and because of them, the writer says, we "only hated him the more." Even our father Jacob chides Joseph for appearing to believe that God told him in a dream that not only his brothers but his mother and father as well would fall down to worship him. Joseph was clearly an obnoxious young man.

And his brothers finally had their fill. When Jacob had sent Joseph out to the pasturelands near Dothan to see if all was well with his older brothers, who were shepherding their father's flocks, the brothers conspired to kill the obnoxious imp, this one who claimed divine visions and the favor of his father. Reuben, thank God, tried to intervene with a plan to save him. But the temptation to sell Joseph into slavery was too great even for Judah. A passing caravan of merchants carrying balm from Gilead to Egypt bought Joseph to resell in Egypt as a slave. We sold our brother into slavery, the text says, for twenty shekels of silver. The compassion within us all, the Reuben that is in us, was overwhelmed with the solution to be rid of our obnoxious brother at a gain of twenty pieces of silver.

"Now Joseph was taken down to Egypt, and Potiphar, an officer of Pharaoh, the captain of the guard, an Egyptian, bought him from the Ishmaelites who had brought him down there. And the Lord was with Joseph." What is this God that abides with slaves? The aggressive qualities which made Joseph obnoxious to his brothers gained for him as a slave to Potiphar the position as overseer of his master's house. And the young man's beauty, his handsomeness, which had no doubt irritated his jealous brothers, attracted or should we say confused poor Potiphar's wife, who had him arrested and imprisoned. And then again we read what is truly the shocking thing about the Bible: "And Joseph's master took him and put him into the prison where the king's prisoners were confined. . . . and the Lord was with Joseph." What is this God who goes to prison? Why doesn't he do what any decent, self-respecting deity ought to do? Why doesn't he send a medium-sized earthquake to crumble the prison walls so the hero can escape? A living God who solves the problems of people, especially good people, would just blast the communists, I mean the Romans, I mean the Egyptians, off the map and save the good guy. Now that would be a god who does what a decent, self-respecting god ought to do. That would be a god you could believe in. You wouldn't call him "dead"! But our poor text says that the biblical God was with Joseph in prison. What a sad, mixed-up Bible. And this is only Genesis. If it carries on like this it'll be trying to tell us that he was with the later Israelite slaves in Egypt, making bricks without straw, or that God too was a POW with the Israelite prisoners in Babylon's dungeons during the Exile, or that when old Herod was killing all the baby boys who might threaten his realm God somehow got down into one of those cradles. Then it'll end up with some story about how God got onto the cross of some teacher charged with blasphemy and sedition against the state. "And he was there in prison, and the Lord was with Joseph . . ."

Joseph's dreams, which had been so offensive to his brothers and even to his parents, and which caused us, his brothers, to sell him into slavery, caused Joseph to become Pharaoh's prime minister and enabled him to instigate a seven-year economic plan which so built Egypt's international credit and balance of payments that when hard days came Egypt was able to go into a foreign aid program rarely equaled until modern times.

You all know the outcome of the story, how Israel's sons made two trips to Egypt to fetch supplies of grain from this stranger, their brother now grown, this prime minister of the Pharaoh, and how Joseph tested their honesty and sincerity, and then how Jacob finally went down with them on their third trip. And you remember that very moving scene when Joseph's love for his brothers caused him to burst into tears with the cry, "I am Joseph your brother, whom you sold into slavery. And now do not be distressed, or angry with yourselves, because you sold me here; for God sent me before you to preserve life. . . . So it was not you who sent me here, but God . . ."

Precisely here is the scandal and the blessing of radical monotheism. Later, when the brothers begged Joseph's forgiveness, fearing that he would hate them and repay them for the evil which they had done him, Joseph replied, "Fear not, for am I in the place of God? As for you, you meant evil against me; but God meant it for good, to bring it about that many people should be kept alive, as they are today." Like his antitype, Jesus in his temptation scenes in the desert and on the cross, Joseph here refused to play god or assume the place of God. Joseph would not forgive his brothers, for that would be presumptuous. Rather, Joseph went on to say the significant thing, "As for you, you meant evil against me; but God meant it for good, to bring it about that many people should be kept alive, as they are today."

Do we know that he who now saves us from starvation is our brother whom we earlier sold into slavery? How can God take such evil and turn it into a blessing? What kind of a God is this who will take our evil, our selling our brother into slavery, and make it our salvation? What kind of a God is this that when we crucify the Son of man he will make that crucifixion our salvation? He who was in prison with Joseph when we sent him there and on the cross in Christ Jesus when we put him there was effecting our salvation through our evil. This is radical monotheism. Not the simplistic, naive notion which Voltaire, Mark Twain, and H. L. Mencken ridiculed, that that which appears evil to us in the hands of a good God is really, in the long view, somehow good. But rather that there is no evil which we commit which is beyond the power of God to redeem. Monotheistic pluralism affirms not the tyranny or despotism of God but rather the sovereignty of God even over evil. The normal human tendency is dualistic polytheism. We much prefer the ancient language of holy war so that we can attribute all evil to some devil or Satan, a rival god, who will in some final cosmic, mythical battle be conquered by the victorious true God. So we still love the language of God's victories over death and evil—as though there were no Bible between us and the ancient Babylonians and Canaanites who affirmed the same victories for their gods every spring.

There are no gods of evil for the true God to conquer either in the Joseph story or in the gospel. I sometimes wonder if we will ever be prepared to hear and understand Peter's sermon at Pentecost in Acts chapter 2: "This Jesus, delivered up according to the definite plan and foreknowledge of God, you [that is, we] crucified and killed by the hands of lawless men. But God raised him up, having loosed the pangs of death because it was not possible for him to be held by it." There is no Mot or Abaddon, no god of death for the true God to fight in order to wrest Jesus from the pangs of death; for the one biblical God is already the God of death as well as of life, the God of light and of darkness, the God of weal and of woe.

The question which usually arises at this point is, Well, if God is the God of evil as well as good, why doesn't he just banish evil? Shoo it away? And here is the fascinating thing about the Bible: its really crucial passages seem to relegate whatever importance holy-war language might finally have to man's battle against his own tendencies toward polytheism. The power that God gives

those who believe that he alone is God is precisely the power to
see that they are now the true sons of God; the redeemed dis-
place the heavenly council of the many gods of man's inchoate
desires. That we are given the power to become the sons of God
simply says again that there are no other sons of God, that is, no
other gods than the one true God who thus summons us to be his
sons. The biblical process of radical monotheism which begins by
humanizing, that is, deposing, all the ancient Near Eastern and
Mediterranean deities in the assertion of the one true God, ends
by setting in their place the true Israel, Christ, the church, the
people of God as his heavenly witnesses.

If we then cannot discount the sovereignty of God in adversity
or in evil, if he is really being God there as well as in what we
would call good, why doesn't he just banish evil? How would he
do so? By fighting evil with evil? That is, by a holy war? No, of
course not, we say, but by taking evil out of the heart of man.
Let everybody be good, we say. No good guys and bad guys—
everybody good. All right. Whose good? The Marxist good? The
capitalist good? The Western good? The Communist good? No,
obviously *the* good, we say, just like in our neighborhood in Lex-
ington. Get rid of the bad guys! And we are precisely back where
we started. We much prefer polytheism: the good God is our god
and the evil god is their god. Of course both or all sides say the
same thing; there is agreement there. Biblical monotheism is so
far ahead of modern man's thinking about good and evil that I
sometimes wonder if we'll ever arrive at the Bible's starting point.
Man's favorite game today seems to be to find evidence against
God, to flunk him out because he doesn't pass our tests of what a
good God ought to be and do. The assumption is that if God
systematically blessed the good guys and blasted the bad guys,
then we would honor him by believing in him. Of course we mean
good and bad from our perspective, naturally. We permit ourselves to call a strike against God when we see the tragedy of the
senseless death of a baby on our streets or in one of our hospitals,
but we honor him with our prayers when babies are burned de-
liberately in some other part of the world because of political
ideology, when we gravely decide that certain babies are better
dead. "Then Herod, when he saw that he had been tricked by the
wise men, was in a furious rage, and he sent and killed all the male

children in Bethlehem and in all that region who were two years old or under, according to the time which he had ascertained from the wise men." Shall we comfortably consider Herod a bad guy? Or is it possible that Herod felt he should crush the rising menace called messianism in order to keep Palestine safe for the Pax Romana? Why didn't God just blast the bad guys, Herod and the Romans, off the map? One suggestion might be that Herod and the Romans represented the responsible world power of the time that was doing a very admirable job of waging the peace of their time and honoring their commitments even in small out-of-the-way countries. I don't know. But what the Bible says is that God himself somehow got down into the cradle of one of those Jew babies at whose neck Herod's sword waged the peace. If Herod and Pilate and the Romans were the bad guys of the time, one wonders who the bad guys are now and in which cradle in which village God is crouching now.

If we sold our brother Joseph into slavery—and the story says we did—and if we honestly don't like being called bad guys—and we don't—and if we have somehow decided that we are kind of glad after all that God doesn't blast the so-called bad guys off the map, sort things out, and generally do what we otherwise have thought any god worth believing in ought to do, then maybe we might catch up to where the Bible starts after all. Where would that put us?

Can we yet believe the Bible that our brother who now saves us is he whom we earlier sold into slavery? Can we somehow believe that those whom we once made slaves can now save us?

What difference does America make? The new historian and the faithful Christian are in complete agreement on the point that history cannot be viewed as a long series of struggles between good guys and bad guys. We who have lived in Jerusalem in modern times know that what Israel calls her War of Independence Palestinians call the Tragedy, and that despite all Zionist propaganda and despite all Arab propaganda there have been only good guys on both sides. We know these things. The white minority of the world are in a particularly favorable circumstance in that while the vast majority of the world's population now think of all colonialists as white devils, evil personified, we are able while scheduling the independence of many colonies to point out the good which imperialism did actually bring to the remotest parts of the world. The historian and the Christian both can state Herod's and Pilate's case: the man in power with a position of responsibility has to get his hands dirty sometimes in order to maintain order, stability, and peace. And I assume that we are also beginning to understand Germany in the thirties to some extent. If we feel we must bomb certain places to contain Communism, we certainly must understand why Stukas had to be sent to strafe Madrid in 1938 when the Communists threatened to take it over. (General Norstad just this January, in the face of world-wide criticisms of our U. S. policy in Vietnam, stated his opinion that the Nuremberg trials were ill founded and indefensible.) We in America on the other hand have an appreciation of true, genuine revolution of the sort of 1776, the model for all since. Our Monroe Doctrine was the finest example of that appreciation, the original intent of which was that all revolutions in Latin America should be free of any foreign influence: let them settle their own affairs. We seem to have forgotten that in our revolution the French sank over a thousand British freighters and actually had more foot soldiers present and accounted for at Yorktown than we colonists did. But by and large it is an admirable thing to affirm with our Monroe Doctrine that revolutions should be free of all foreign interference—though of course we do not thereby mean to be ungrateful to France.

But what difference does America make? What lasting contribution can we make to the great world revolution which we had the honor and privilege (all deference and regard to George III, of course) of starting? America has worked hard in the chancelleries of the world for effecting the independence of Asian and African countries from their former European colonists, mainly I suppose because we know what it means to be free of them ourselves. What is the difference between us and all those European colonial powers, from ancient Greece and Rome down to Great Britain? Carl Oglesby has written:

> It seems to me that America has a much better chance to understand [the world revolution] than did England or France, because America, uniquely, has a third-world nation within herself: the community of American Negroes. When we read of Bull Connor

we can learn something about Diem and Ky. When we read of Julian Bond, we can learn something about Ahmed Ben Bella. White Americans have an unparalleled opportunity to learn first-hand about the origins of this turbulence that vexes us in the world. We can learn that revolution comes from the casting off of slavery, and that slavery comes from masters; that it is not the rebels who produce the troubles of the world, but those troubles that produce the rebels.*

You may recall that Pogo once pointed out with respect to a certain verse in Isaiah that the lion is quite willing to lie down with the lamb; it's the lamb that won't hold still.

James Baldwin in "Black Man in America" has also said that unlike the situation in the colonial states in Africa and Asia, the white man here is not a colonist (at least not any longer) for the red Indian or the black African to drive out, but white, red, and black are all involved in each other.

Are we a people more concerned about law and order and property rights than about justice and human rights? No, said Peter Howard, the late British leader of Moral Rearmament. "The different races in America are her strength and glory. They are an asset no other country possesses. . . . My faith," he continued, "is in modern America. . . . I believe those who have been victims of the worst discrimination will be the first to heal the hates and fears of others because they themselves are free from fear and hate. . . . Those who have passed through the fires of persecution can hold forth one hand to persecutors and persecuted alike, and with the other uplift a flame of freedom to illuminate the earth. . . . It remains my belief," he said, "that crossless Christians do more to camouflage the reality of Christ's revolution for humanity than any Communist or Fascist."†

But it was Martin Luther King, Jr., answering the eight southern churchmen in a long letter from prison in a Birmingham jail on 16 April 1963, who interpreted Joseph for us today.

I hope the church as a whole will meet the challenge of this decisive hour. But even if the church does not come to the aid of justice, I have no despair about the future. I have no fear about

*Carl Oglesby, *Christianity and Revolution* 2 (1966): 21.
†Peter Howard, *New York Times,* 29 March 1964, p. 10E.

the outcome of our struggle in Birmingham, even if our motives are presently misunderstood. We will reach the goal of freedom in Birmingham and all over the nation, because the goal of America is freedom. Abused and scorned though we may be, our destiny is tied up with America's destiny. Before the Pilgrims landed at Plymouth, we were here. Before the pen of Jefferson etched the majestic words of the Declaration of Independence across the pages of history, we were here. For more than two centuries our forebears labored in this country without wages; they made cotton king; they built the homes of their masters while suffering gross injustice and shameful humiliation—and yet out of a bottomless vitality they continued to thrive and develop. If the inexpressible cruelties of slavery could not stop us, the opposition we now face will surely fail. We will win our freedom because the sacred heritage of our nation and the eternal will of God are embodied in our echoing demands. . . . Let us all hope that the dark clouds of racial prejudice will soon pass away and the deep fog of misunderstanding will be lifted from our fear-drenched communities, and in some not too distant tomorrow the radiant stars of love and brotherhood will shine over our great nation with all their scintillating beauty. Yours for the cause of Peace and Brotherhood,

MARTIN LUTHER KING, JR.*

Are we Christian enough really to believe that God can redeem the evil we have done? Can we believe that those whom we sold into slavery can be our salvation? It is evil, evil, evil to sell one's brother into slavery. But can we believe that he whom we sold to Caesar can be our Savior?

"When Joseph's brothers saw that their father was dead, they said, 'It may be that Joseph will hate us and pay us back for all the evil which we did to him.' So they sent a message to Joseph, saying, '. . . Forgive, we pray you, the transgression of your brothers and their sin. . . .' Joseph wept when they spoke to him . . . and said to them, 'Fear not, for am I in the place of God? As for you, you meant evil against me; but God meant it for good, to bring it about that many people should be kept alive, as they are today.' "

*Martin Luther King, Jr., "Letter from Birmingham Jail," *Why We Can't Wait* (New York: Harper & Row Publishers, 1963), pp. 97–98. Copyright © 1963 by Martin Luther King, Jr. Reprinted by permission.

3. Go Tell Them I'll Be There

"Go Tell Them I'll Be There" was preached in the Brick Church in Rochester, New York, on the first Sunday in Advent, 28 November 1965. It was our first trip back to our old home after moving the previous July to New York City. We had looked forward to it with keen anticipation, especially our son, Robin, who had grown up in Rochester and in the Brick Church.

I had already begun to think about the significance of the burning bush in Exodus 3 for understanding the church. My file still contains my earliest notes on the ideas which launched the sermon. It was where Moses first met Yahweh, according to the so-called Elohist source (Exodus 3), and it was the place where the liberated slaves would meet after the Exodus to worship God. Exod. 3:12 says that the worship event would be the "sign" that God had sent Moses. The same notes in longhand include the following: "The burning bush was not consumed, precisely because of God's presence in it. The locus of the presence of God, that place to which we turn aside from shepherding our sheep, the place where we remove our sandals—the church—may be quite unidentifiable as such. It may be but a scrawny Sinaitic bush on a desolate hillside or it may appear, like the inner city, to be burning down. It is the place of God's presence, from which God calls to us, where reverence is due him, where God reveals his name, where he gives us a mission, and to which we shall return. Even so Moses had two questions for God at the bush before he would accept the mission: who am I, and who shall I say sent me? God's sovereignty is best expressed in his freedom. Yahweh was not a local deity only but was free to cross borders to champion the dispossessed: God's freedom is his universal sovereignty." Those were the kernels from which the following grew.

"Go Tell Them I'll Be There" is in a sense the third of a triology preached in the Brick Church: "The Banquet of the Dispossessed" (chapter 5 below) on 31 August 1964, "Promise and Providence" (chapter 1 above) on 23 May 1965, and this one on 28 November 1965—incidentally, my thirty-eighth birthday. The first came at the end of the hottest summer Rochester had ever known, the riots of 1964, and the second after a year of dissension in the Rochester churches over Saul Alinsky's being engaged by the Council of Churches following the riots to help the black community of Rochester organize.

This third sermon was for Advent. Where was God acting in the world? Where could you find him? Who was he? Who were we? The biblical answer to them all seemed to be "Go tell them I'll be there." The people shall have the power to be free. They will be enabled to worship God "in this place," to serve him and not Pharaoh. That is the freedom of God which he gives, by his grace, to those who hear the message and believe that he is coming.

Exodus 3:4, 7–8, 11–14

There are two traditions reported in the Bible concerning the occasion of Moses' first encounter with Yahweh, the God of ancient Israel. In the one account God speaks to Moses from a burning bush and in the other from before a mountain crevasse, but the conversations between the shepherd and the deity in both passages are remarkably similar. In Exodus 3 and in Exodus 33 God commissioned Moses to go to the slaves in Egypt with the message "Go tell them I'll be there."

The longer tradition in Exodus 3 is the better known. It tells of the numinous experience of Moses in pursuing his curiosity about a mountain bush that burned without being consumed. This Moses of Israelite parentage had grown up in Pharaoh's household in Egypt. As Pharaoh's adopted grandson, Moses came to learn that the slaves called Israelites were his own people, and in this manner were the eyes of one of Pharaoh's own family opened to the injustice of the power structure of Egypt. (For in truth none is as blind to certain forms of injustice as the responsible, established authority of any society.) Only when Moses could identify with the bottom of Egypt's social structure, only when he could say, "They are my people," did he see the injustice of the economic system by which he had benefited all his life.

But once his eyes were thus opened, Moses acted. His passion for open justice, the justice which can pervade society from its upper levels all the way through its lowest, brought him to civil and criminal disobedience. Seeing an Egyptian taskmaster beating a Hebrew slave, Moses killed the Egyptian and became a fugitive from justice out in the Midianite desert and grazing wastes of Sinai.

In that quiet pastoral setting a strange thing happened. A bush burned for this escaped murderer; it burned and continued to burn. God spoke to Moses in that experience and in effect told him that he, like Moses, identified with the bottom of the social scale in Egypt. This is biblical anthropopathism at its best. God suffered the injustice of Egyptian justice. He told Moses that he knew their sufferings and that he had come to deliver the dispossessed whom he had chosen as his own people. He then commissioned Moses to be his agent for salvation.

But before Moses accepted the commission he asked two questions. The two questions are put differently in the two traditions but in essence they are the same in each: "Who am I?" Moses asked of God, "and who are you?"

In Exodus 3, the so-called Elohist account, Moses asks, "Who am I that I should go to Pharaoh and bring the sons of Israel out of Egypt?" The answer is immediate and unequivocal, "I indeed will be with you." Similarly in Exodus 33, the so-called Yahwist account, when Moses says, "But thou hast not let me know whom thou wilt send with me," the answer is equally immediate and clear: "My presence will go with you." Moses' first question in the two accounts is in effect one question. For though they are phrased quite differently, the answer to Moses' first query in both accounts is the same: "I will be with you." Therefore Moses' request in Exodus 33 to know who will accompany him evokes the same response as his question of self-identity, his "Who am I?" in Exodus 3. The question "What credentials have I to challenge the economic and social system of the most powerful nation in the known world?" is in effect the same as the question "Who will be our guide? What force or power will validate this freedom movement from the securities of the injustice of Egypt to the insecurities of the desert of freedom?" For the answer to both questions is the same: "Even I will be with you: my presence will go with you." The answer to the question "Who am I?"—*if* it is a true question, not an idle question, but a legitimate question in terms of the uncertainties life demands and the risks God summons us to take to challenge the system—the answer, the only answer worth considering, comes not in the human terms of our various *data vitae* but in the divine terms of God's transcendent humility. When you face the Pharaoh not for yourself but like Moses as a man for others, and when you face the bleak heat and thirst of the desert not for yourself but for the poor souls whom you've led out there, you know existentially that the true answer to the question of identity must transcend the available historical evidence. The only answer that can hold up for the dissenter in Pharaoh's court or the advocate and leader of a new way of life out on the bare desert heights is and must be *Immanuel*. And when the Pharaoh's heart seems to be hard and he argues that you're moving too fast, and when the very ones you've led to freedom complain that the "way out" (the exodus) is too rough, there's only one identity worth having: *Immanuel*, precisely the presence of him who comes and will come, of him in whose hands gently sift the sands of time, who alone can see that Egypt—for all her power and magnificence and wealth and willingness to share out of her storehouses with the hungry of the world—who alone can know that Egypt's way (the way of Pharaoh) is false even though all the evidence points to the contrary. *Immanuel* is the biblical answer to every valid quest for identity.

Moses' other question is equally important. In Exodus 3 he asks, "When they ask me, 'What is his name?' what shall I tell them?" In Exodus 33 he says to God, "Show me thy ways," or "Show me thy glory." They are really one question: "Who are you?" And the divine answers given in the two accounts are basically one answer. "I am who I am" in Exodus 3 and "I will be gracious to whom I will be gracious" in Exodus 33 are similar in that they both affirm God's freedom.

When Moses asked, "Who am I that I should be the agitator for Israel's Freedom Now movement?" God answered, "I will be with you." St. Paul, that astounding student of the Bible, said even to the unbelieving Athenians on the Areopagus, "He is not far from each one of us, for in him we live and move and have our being." The Bible is amazingly consistent at the point of its answer to the question of our self-identity, to the question of our existence.

When Jeremiah asked God the same question, of why should he who was only a lad go forth to speak in God's name, the answer again was "I will be with you." And the fellowship of God was the one thing of which Job was sure and in all his suffering refused to deny. Man is derivative of God, and without him there is no biblical answer to the question of who we are. In the second account Moses himself pressed God on this point, and in Exod. 33:16 we have what is probably the heart of all biblical theology, "Is it not in thy going with us," Moses insisted of God, "that we are distinct, I and thy people, from all other peoples on the face of the earth?" The abiding presence and fellowship of God is precisely our identity. The name which the prophet Isaiah gave to the child of Israel's hope is my name, is your name, is the name of the presence of God among men, *Immanuel*, "God with us."

Exodus 33 offers an etymology of the divine name Yahweh based on the ancient Semitic root which implies that God is a passionate God, a loving God who claims for himself what he loves—a compassionate God who, while just, is forgiving. The name Yahweh, the Lord, according to one view means "I am passionate in that I am passionate."* The usual translation here is "I will be gracious to whom I will be gracious, and will show mercy on whom I will show mercy." And that is correct too; but one misses the point if he does not see that the subject and the predicate are the same. God is absolutely free. God is indeed loving, merciful, and forgiving, but love is not caprice, mercy is not whim, and forgiveness comes only in a framework of justice. But this is the God whose nature it is to be passionate; he is a jealous God whose love is not challenged by the wills of other gods; he is a judging, redeeming God. It is he who elects, it is he who chooses, it is he who judges, it is he who saves by his passion. God's answer in Exodus 33 to Moses' question of who God is, is the very wood of the cross of Jesus Christ. But the other answer to Moses' question of who God is, in Exodus 3, is the very stone of the crude cradle of Bethlehem's birth. Here the etymology is based on the ancient Semitic root meaning "to be." It states that God is. Exodus 3 does not deny God's passion for man, for this

*S. D. Goitein, "*YHWH* the Passionate, the Monotheistic Meaning and Origin of the Name *YHWH*," *Vetus Testamentum* 6 (1956): 1–9.

is the tradition which earlier states that God knows the suffering of Pharaoh's slaves, but it affirms a new dimension to our understanding of God: "I am in that I am." He is the God who is. He is the only God who is. He is being itself, according to the earliest Greek translators of this passage. And the Hebrew means that and much more. Professor W. F. Albright, among others, says it means, "I am he who brings into being, or creates"; and it may mean that as well. But it reaches much deeper. For as in the etymology in Exodus 33 the subject and the predicate are cognate. God is in that he is. God's being is in God's being. He is absolutely free. One cannot finally say simply that God is, any more than he can say that God is not. God is the dimension which includes creating and being, in which creation and being are, in which we live and move and have being. And God is the dimension which includes not-being. He is the God of light and darkness, good and evil, life and death. Our son, Robin, claims that when back in the second grade he appeared in school to be daydreaming, he was really thinking about what is and why it is not.

God's nature as freedom is nowhere better seen than in Genesis 1:26, the *imago dei* passage, in which we may steal a glimpse of God himself. The image of God in man is there explained as man's freedom with respect to all the forces of nature. "That he may have dominion over or be a king with respect to the fish of the sea, the birds, etc." is not a proof text for food gathering or for the explorations of science but an antipolytheistic argument of man's relation to God as well as to all else in the created order. It is the same as our Lord said in the Sermon on the Mount: to seek or to commit oneself first to the kingdom or sovereignty or absolute freedom of God is to have "all these things" added to him, that is, he is free of the tyranny of all these things, of all forces of creation. Similarly Paul said that in Christ Jesus all things are ours. Manifestly it is not a question either in the New Testament or in the Old Testament of possession of all these things or of dominion over birds or the like but rather of man's appointed ability regally to reflect in himself, though dimly, God's absolute freedom from the tyranny and power of all things in creation. Genesis 1:26 affords a glimpse of God's essential nature of freedom and affirms man's essential and potential freedom of all false gods or claims upon him. Who am I? asked the fugitive of the bush, and who are you?

"I am that I am" in Exodus 3 means that God is absolutely free of any predicate which man might attach to "I am." To put it crudely, God can applaud the thinking of the death-of-God theologians because he knows that they also are telling the truth about him. The God which orthodoxy or conservatism thinks it has syntaxed in its creeds and its doctrines just doesn't syntax. Ancient Israel's ark of the covenant never contained God: it was but a symbol of his presence. We have no difficulty in affirming the judging sovereignty and freedom of the God of Genesis and Exodus over the death-of-God theologies, just as we have no difficulty in affirming his sovereignty over and freedom from any theology. He is the Judge Pantocrator of every creed, every dogma, every doctrine, every metaphor, and every tenet by which man attempts to understand him. Even the dogma of his not-being cannot contain him. If you know the God of the Bible you know it would be just like him to start such a rumor. Who am I? asked the fugitive of the bush, and who are you?

For God is even free of freedom. He is precisely free to love, to judge, to redeem, to save, to suffer what man suffers, to know our sufferings, as he told Moses in Exodus 3. It is often said that the death-of-God theologians owe much of their thinking to the German Christian martyr of the Second World War Dietrich Bonhoeffer, who in one of his letters from a Nazi prison wrote that "God allows himself to be edged out of the world and onto the cross."* But he also in the same letters from prison affirmed his understanding of God's freedom of the universe, his being outside it, for in criticizing Bultmann's existentialism Bonhoeffer also said, "God is the 'beyond' in the midst of our life."

The Bible says that God in all his majestic and sovereign holiness has come to live among men, granting his presence. It is with such ideas that the Bible starts. Genesis 1 speaks of the Creator God whose majesty and power are beyond all our vain imaginings, but Genesis 2 speaks of his walking in the garden of

---

*Dietrich Bonhoeffer, *Prisoner for God* (New York: Macmillan Publishing Co., 1958), p. 164.

man's first abode calling on Adam and Eve, paying them a visit. Genesis 11 speaks of the total impossibility of man's vain hope of attaining unto heaven of his own devising, but Genesis 12 speaks of God in intimate conversation with a man. The Bible starts with God and not with what I can believe about him. The Bible does not take its point of departure with man's capacity for belief. It does not start with man's belief in God, it starts with God's belief in man. Who am I? asked the fugitive of the bush, and who are you?

One cannot begin where the Bible begins without God. The Bible is not greatly interested in whether man can adjudge its truth worthy of his belief; it unequivocally says that it is man being judged worthy or unworthy of God's belief in him. And the first reality apprehended in the presence of God is his judgment of us. But it is not so much that we do not measure up to his majesty or to his purity or to his holiness; all that is rather obvious, I suppose. The most stringent judgment upon us in the presence of God is that we cannot measure up to his humility—for the Bible is essentially a story of divine humility. His majesty is assumed and often affirmed, but the story is about God's presence among men and not among heavenly beings; in other words the story is about such humility that no one escapes the judgment of it. God has stooped to conquer us by love. He has granted his presence among us. Who am I? asked the fugitive of the bush, and who are you?

"What is the truth?" asked Pilate of our Lord at his trial. And he did not answer, for truth is judgment, divine judgment: It is the judgment of the condemned on the accuser, of the oppressed on the oppressor, of tomorrow's discovery on today's ignorance. It is the saving judgment of the Ultimate on all our penultimas. It is the silence of God's Christ in the presence of our Pilate.

I sometimes wonder if we are fully aware of how subversive and revolutionary the Bible is. Careful study of the Bible in its historical and political setting is disturbing, not comforting. Those who try to say that studying the Bible is an escape from reality simply have not studied it. For here is a story from beginning to end of judgment, that is, of turning things upside down and inside out. Judgment in the Bible means the saving judgment of God's presence—his government and rule, his way of doing things, not ours. He challenges the victorious and comforts the defeated; he indicts the righteous and forgives the sinner. In celebrations of victory the biblical God seeks out the defeated. In every Jewish home throughout the world in the solemn and joyous ceremony at the Passover table, a drop of red wine will fall on every plate in memory of Egyptians who at the Exodus drowned thirty-three hundred years ago that Israel might be free. The Bible is the book which explains election as humility, pride as vanity, success as an aspect of defeat, and blessing as an occasion for sin: it expresses a plaguing love that will not let us go. We somehow think God should honor our efforts on his behalf; instead God always seems to come up with another question, another challenge. The biblical God is strange, impertinent, and offensive to those who think they are right; for he has a way of showing us what is wrong about what is right. The biblical doctrine of divine providence is the biblical doctrine of divine judgment. The Bible did not simply continue in the ancient Babylonian and Hittite views that a people's god was of necessity a guiding and protecting deity. The Bible turned the common theology of the Ancient Near East upside down and declared that on the contrary the true God is a judging, challenging God whose elect people or whose elect one bears in his body the unjust wounds and scars of transcendent righteousness. The Bible says that a group of responsible, law-abiding Americans called Romans and a group of responsible, God-fearing Presbyterians and Methodists called Pharisees did the best they could in a complicated situation involving delicate international relations and decided that for the good of both church and state a certain messianic pretender and rabble-rouser from Galilee should be dealt capital punishment. But in that situation we are told God identified with, God took *his* identity in the accused. Who am I? asked the fugitive of the bush, and who are you?

The God who entered the huts and hovels of Pharaoh's slaves in Egypt is probably today in the huts and hovels of Vietnamese peasants. The God who spoke from the burning bush might be speaking today from a jungle aflame. The God who served as Israel's guide in the desert of newfound freedom may be serving as our guide in our desert of newfound freedoms. And we may find, as those freed slaves found, that he is not dead but rather has gone on three days' journey ahead of us. And we may also find, when our postmodern freedoms from the past have lost their lustre, that God has not weaned or abandoned us after all. The God who directed Nebuchadnezzar to take Israel into exile and then joined them himself in Babylon's dungeons and jails might be with us yet (*Immanuel*) in the refugee camps of the world. The God who got down into the cradle of a baby Jew threatened by Herod's sword is still known in a world threatening its own destruction. And the God who got on the cross of a man trapped in the justice of the combination of the two best legal systems of antiquity, the Hebraic and the Roman, surely is yet known in our justice, in Birmingham and Saigon. Is not the presence of him who told Egypt's ancient slaves "I'll be there" known also in a society whose government frenetically pursues draft-card burners but must for delicate legal reasons remain silent when a soldier-murderer is acquitted, and when human torches speak to us of the murders which for delicate political reasons we are daily committing abroad? Who am I? they asked the stranger, and who are you?*

*The experience of the discovery of the empty tomb gives rise to the same sorts of questions of identity as Moses' discovery of the burning bush. (Cf. Mark 16:5).

4. What Happened at Nazareth?

"What Happened at Nazareth?" was delivered in the Riverside Church in New York City on 20 June 1971. It was picked up by recording from the radio broadcast and distributed by Thesis Theological Cassettes, vol. 2, no. 10 (1971), soon after; this is its first publication in print.

I shall never forget the occasion, not so much because it was the only time I've preached at Riverside, but because Abraham Heschel was present. His entrance was rather more dramatic than that of the principals involved in the service, despite all the pomp which accompanied processionals at Riverside. He was late, having put in some hours' work earlier that morning in his study at the Jewish Theological Seminary. He followed the stream of ushers in the eastern aisle of the nave as they marched down with full plates to the increasing crescendo of Frederic Swann's version of the Old Hundredth. Heedless of the scene he was creating he kept peering right and left to see where I was in the chancel so he could sit on the side from which I would preach. We had hoped he could come but were not at all sure because of the enormous demands on his time. Despite our close relationship and our having talked at length on several matters the previous week, I could not bring myself to tell him I was preaching that day, so Dora, my wife, told Sylvia to inform her husband. Dora and Sylvia are intimate friends and piano partners. Heschel actually sat on the wrong side and when he discovered his mistake, again heedless of all the ritual taking place he walked right through the rigid line of ushers to the west side nearer the pulpit.

At that point my good friend Gene Laubach, who conducted the service that day in Ernest Campbell's absence, leaned over to me and indicating Heschel whispered that the church had received calls earlier in the week from some radical group warning of their intention to conduct a demonstration that morning, and that the strange little man in the white beard might well try to take over the pulpit. (Riverside had had many incidents since 1968, and under the leadership of Ernest Campbell had conducted itself well indeed.) I leaned back over to Gene and assured him that if that man wanted to take the pulpit I would be honored and usher him up to it myself. Poor Gene, I am sure, wished the floor under him would gently open to some escape when I told him who that man was.

My sermon was about an incident in a synagogue at Nazareth. The synagogue preacher that day had been invited to read a scripture portion, so it had not been a question of his taking over the pulpit. His remarks on the Isaiah portion were at first well received, but his sermon on it incited the congregation to near riot.

The question was why. I was not satisfied either with the moralistic homilies I had heard on the passage or with scholarly treatises on it which seemed to avoid the main issue. A full scholarly treatment of the basic ideas in my sermon appeared four years later, titled "From Isaiah 61 to Luke 4," in *Christianity, Judaism and Other Greco-Roman Cults*, ed. Jacob Neusner, pt. 1, *New Testament* (Leiden: E. J. Brill, 1975), pp. 75–106.

Jesus' sermon theologizes rather than moralizes. I do not think that either Jesus or Luke intended to exhort readers to give alms to foreigners and outsiders. Such a program may well be a good program of obedience based upon reflection on the passage. But it became clear to me in working on the passage in the light of the rest of Luke and of the rest of the New Testament that the point was theological. Jesus' own hermeneutics were those of the freedom of the God of grace. God is free to elect whom he will, and when all is said and done and truth is fully told (at the eschaton) God will be free to take his blessings to whom he thinks best. Like many another passage in Luke and indeed in the Bible, this passage attacks closed systems of meritocracy. Even the faithful can see that divine grace is a form of divine injustice when it is directed to those outside the church. Pursuit of the integrity of reality is a challenge throughout life, not a game, and Luke's version of Jesus' first sermon underscores the realism of it. Once that is perceived then programs of sharing the means and wealth of the church and of Christians with non-Christians may be well conceived.

1 Kings 17:8–16; Isaiah 61:1–2
Luke 4:16–30

The Gospel lesson of the morning is commonly called "The Sermon at Nazareth." Luke presents the episode of this sermon delivered in Jesus' home church, or synagogue, as the first act of his ministry.

For understanding the whole of the mission and ministry of Jesus Luke ranks this homecoming occasion at Nazareth as next in importance to the Passion account at the end of the Gospel. The one stood at the start of Jesus' ministry and the other at its end. Luke saw in what happened at Nazareth a key to the Passion of Christ: in his account of this event Luke provides an early answer to the question of why Jesus was crucified.

Luke tells us of Jesus' going to the lectern in the synagogue and reading from the book of Isaiah, and then records the actual passage read from Isaiah. He then reports that Jesus said upon closing the scroll, "Today is this scripture fulfilled in your ears." It is here that Luke says the people would have said to Jesus, "Physician, heal yourself," which for Luke was comparable to the centurion and bad thief's shouting to Jesus on the cross, "Save yourself and us." Luke then records the essence of the midrash or sermon which Jesus preached and the congregation's reaction to it as they dragged Jesus out to the brow of the hill on which the city was built to throw him down to be stoned. And here is where Luke's account of the Nazareth incident differs most significantly from that of his colleagues': whereas in Mark and Matthew it is Jesus who rejected the congregation at Nazareth because of their lack of faith, in Luke it is the faithful of Nazareth who rejected Jesus because he had apparently committed blasphemy.

Luke forces us by his account to ask the question, What happened at Nazareth? Why did the good, faithful churchgoers of Nazareth, many of them Jesus' cousins and members of his immediate family, turn from respectable citizens into a lynching mob? What changed them from admirers, at the point where Jesus had completed the reading from Isaiah, into a hateful mob seeking his death? Not only does Luke force the question, he goes to great pains to provide the answer—and the answer to why the responsible folk of Nazareth wanted to lynch Jesus here at the start of his ministry provides a key, I think, to Luke's understanding of why the responsible leaders of Jerusalem sought to crucify him at the end.

In order to seek Luke's answer to this question we must as we study the account keep in mind five crucial points:

1. The four Gospels and Paul—indeed most of the New Testament—are eschatological, so as scholars from Albert Schweitzer down to Richard Hiers have insisted, the gospel cannot be reduced simply to a set of guidelines for an ongoing program. The word eschaton means the end of history, or of time, as we know it. Eschaton for us therefore means at least something like "in the final analysis" or "the final truth."

2. Luke presents Jesus as an eschatological prophet. This does not mean simply that he proclaimed the eschaton to be near. A prophet in the Bible is one who interprets the identifying and life-giving tradition of the believing community (in this instance the passage from Isaiah) as a challenge for his contemporaries. As R. G. Collingwood said of the artist, the prophet "tells his audience, at the risk of their displeasure, the secrets of their own hearts. . . . As spokesman of his community, the secrets he must utter are theirs . . . [for] no community altogether knows its own heart . . ." (cf. Luke 2:35). Especially is it ignorant of the worst disease of the human mind, says Collingwood, the corruption of consciousness. The prophet must in the light of God's final truth reveal the corruption of consciousness of his own community. In other words by studying the manner by which the prophets, including Jesus, interpreted their traditions in their day we can arrive at a rule for the way *we* should interpret Scripture in our day; and the first such rule would be "Whenever our reading of a biblical passage makes us feel self-righteous, we can be confident we have misread it."

3. If, then, Jesus was an eschatological prophet, as I think Luke presents him, his message was not just that the final truth was near but that even in the final analysis *that* truth would be a challenge to Israel's or the church's self-understanding.

4. In order to be able really to appreciate what Jesus said, we must in reading the New Testament identify with those to whom he spoke. The greatest falsehood in the church's usual reading of the Gospels is that it somehow assumes it is better than first-century Judaism and has progressed closer to the final truth. This may be true in certain superficial ways in comparing the first

century to the twentieth, but the simple historical truth is that
the human mind is no more able to discern its own corruption of
consciousness today than it was in the first century. To put it another way there is not one thing Jesus said to the people of his
day which is outdated for us today—*if* we read it correctly. And
reading the Nazareth episode correctly means first and foremost
identifying with the good congregation in attendance. If we do
so, I suggest that we may have put ourselves in a position to find
the answer to the question of what happened at Nazareth.

5. Finally, in reading the passage we must try to find a dynamic
analogy in our day to what Jesus said at Nazareth in the first
century. Normally in reading or seeing a story on TV or in the
movies we identify almost unconsciously with the good guy and
thus set up in our minds the situation the writer intended. But
history cannot be read that way, nor especially can the Bible. The
truth of history reaches us only when read by dynamic analogy.
In order to recover the truth of any historic event we must breathe
into it the normal tensions of the present—that is, we must attribute to it the ambiguity of reality. History should not be read and
the Bible must not be read by static analogy: truth is not available by assuming good guys and bad guys. The truth of history is
present tension. That is, once we have determined what in the
first century made the Nazareth congregation angry, we still have
not understood the passage. Not until we have sensed in ourselves
the tension between Jesus and that congregation and can feel in
ourselves their indignant anger at him have we really understood
the answer Luke gives to the question, What happened at Nazareth that day that turned a respectable congregation into a lynching mob?

Luke's answer is crystal clear: it was Jesus' sermon. Luke rivets
our attention on the sermon. After Jesus had read the Scripture
lesson from Isaiah, all eyes were turned expectantly on him. We
now know that he could not have read a passage of more explosive
interest than this one from Isaiah 61. It was the going passage of
the time because it spoke of *how* the eschaton would take place.
It speaks of the coming of a herald to proclaim the acceptable
year of God for the poor, captives, blind, and oppressed.

We now know because of a recent discovery among the Dead Sea Scrolls that this passage from Isaiah was a crucial one for many Palestinians of the first century as a key to the eschaton. Some Jewish sects apparently called themselves the Poor, with a capital P as it were, so convinced were they that this and similar passages applied to themselves, and they described how God would bless *them* when the eschaton arrived. We now know from the Dead Sea Scrolls that the Essenes, whose chief occupation it appears was meditating on and interpreting Scripture, and waiting for the eschaton, always understood that the blessings of the Old Testament would apply to themselves in the eschaton whereas the judgments would befall their enemies, whether the Hasmoneans in Jerusalem, the Romans, or all the cosmic forces of evil.

The Essenes, incidentally, had a very orthodox doctrine of sin: they daily confessed their manifold sins and wickedness which they from time to time committed against God's divine majesty. But nowhere in the scores of documents we now have from the eleven Qumran caves do the Essenes interpret Scripture as a judgment on themselves or as a challenge to *their* ways of thinking about themselves. In this regard they were a normal denomination.

And we can be sure the same views obtained among the faithful of Nazareth. It had been a century since the Romans, those ancient European colonialists, had taken over Palestine, exacting taxes and depriving the people of their freedoms. Where else in the world did you need to look for the poor and the dispossessed of whom Isaiah spoke? Crushed under the Roman heel and clamped in the claws of the Roman eagle the good, faithful synagogue-goers of Palestine of A.D. 25 had about had it. They must have figured that perhaps at no time in Jewish history was their own situation more comparable to that of their ancestors, the original slaves in Egypt whom God had redeemed from Pharaoh's oppression.

Thus when Jesus not only read from *the* crucial passage in Isaiah but immediately thereafter made the bald proclamation "Today this scripture is fulfilled in your ears," a phrase which appears only here in all the Bible, there would have been an electric-shock wave passing through the congregation: This is it.

The herald is here. This is the year we get rid of these damned Romans. Shocked, though not surprised, the congregation was also puzzled. Someone asked, "Isn't that Joe's boy?" They clearly liked the words about God's grace which he had read from Isaiah and which, they assumed, applied to them. They liked what they heard him say about today being the day, but they were not sure of him, a local boy. Like the Essenes they had become convinced perhaps that the herald would be a heavenly figure, quite identifiable as such.

Jesus then quoted them a very old proverb which provides the key to what happened at Nazareth and to what Luke is trying to tell us about it: "No prophet is acceptable in his own country." Mark and Matthew at this point cite the proverb in another form: "A prophet is not without honor save in his own country." But we know, in part from an ancient papyrus, that Luke gave the correct form of the proverb: "No prophet is acceptable in his own country."

But in this passage the proverb does *not* mean what at first blush it appears to mean, namely, that the people would have accepted Jesus as the herald of good news *if* he had been from somewhere else. One has to ask *why* a prophet is not acceptable in his own country. All Old Testament prophets had been from Israel; all of them had been Israelites or Jews. No prophet was ever a visiting fireman from outside the covenant community, and this proverb applies to the Old Testament judgmental prophets perfectly. Amos was run out of town. Isaiah was teased and chided. Jeremiah was scorned and tried twice for blasphemy and sedition. It was to this history of prophetic interpretation of Israel's tradition, her Torah, that Jesus pointed in citing this proverb. Why can no prophet be acceptable amongst his own people? Because a true prophet in the biblical tradition so interpreted Scripture or tradition as to emphasize the challenge it brought to the very group that found its identity in that tradition. The proverb in the form Luke gives it provides the key because it contains, in Greek, the very word on which the Isaiah Scripture passage Jesus read had ended—the word *dektos,* meaning "acceptable": The herald was to proclaim the *acceptable* year of the Lord. No prophet is *acceptable* in his own country.

What Isaiah meant, and what Jesus knew he meant, was a year or a time acceptable to God. In other words the message of a true prophet is to proclaim what is the will of God, not what is the will of men. All the more so is this true of the eschatological prophet who proclaims the final truth in the light of which *all* our proximate truths are judged for their true worth. What will happen on that great gettin'-up morning or, if you prefer, in the final analysis, will be what pleases God, i.e., what is really truth, not necessarily what pleases us who think we believe in God; it will expose our views of truth for the shallow things they are. If we knew what we were doing we would find the prayer "Not my will but thine be done" the toughest prayer we could utter. If we do not find it so, it is probably because no one has been indiscreet enough (that is, prophetic enough) to expose before us our *own* corruption of consciousness.

Another Isaiah put it another way: God's ways are not our ways and his thoughts are not our thoughts (Isa. 55:8). But we corrupt that to read, "God's ways are not their ways . . ." and remain ignorant of the secrets of our own heart. It is what we have also done with the message of the angels in the Bethlehem story in Luke 2:14. The church has changed it to read—and it did so very early on—"Glory to God in the highest and on earth peace, goodwill among men." Its original meaning is "Glory to God in the highest and on earth peace to men acceptable to God." But like the congregation at Nazareth we figure that what is acceptable to us is what is acceptable to God.

It must be stressed that the faithful at Nazareth were no more selfish in thinking this way, no more mistaken in their theology, than we are. Their interpretation of Scripture, like that of the Essenes, the Pharisees, and our own, was normal. After all, what's the use of being faithful if God does not intend to honor our efforts on his behalf? This stuff in the Gospel about paying those who labor only one hour at the end of the day the same as those of us who have borne the burden of the day and the scorching heat (Matt. 20:12) is birdseed. We in the church love the sentiment in the parable of the prodigal son until we realize that what it says is that God is running down the road at the end of the story to embrace somebody else. We dearly weep at the force of the idea of how the angels rejoice over the finding of the one lost sheep until we realize they're singing about somebody else. And we in the church have corrupted it by assuming that the lost sheep was coming to his senses by coming into the church— joining the in-group. But that is not what the text says. It says that when the final day arrives (translate "when the final truth is out"), the great joy will be for outsiders, foreigners, the unchurched. By now we too ought to be asking, Well, what's the use of being in church now?

And that is exactly what the good folk at Nazareth were asking when Jesus had finished his sermon. And by dynamic analogy that sermon ought to offend us just as much as it offended our antecedents at Nazareth. What happened at Nazareth? Here is what happened. Jesus preached a sermon on the Isaiah 61 passage by telling two biblical stories.

"In truth I tell you, there were many widows in Israel in the days of Elijah; but Elijah was sent to none of them, but only to Zarephath, in the land of Sidon, to a woman who was a widow. And there were many lepers in Israel in the time of the prophet Elisha; but none of them was cleansed, only Naaman the Syrian" (Luke 4:25–27; cf. 1 Kings 17 and 2 Kings 5).

The Isaiah 61 passage would itself have caused the people to think of Elijah, who according to tradition was to return as the eschatological prophet to proclaim the acceptable year of the Lord. Elijah was the symbol of the beginning of the end. However, by reminding the people of what the book of 1 Kings says the historical Elijah was really like—that is, the troubler of ancient Israel who challenged Israel's own narrow views of God— Jesus clearly angered his audience.

And Luke reports everybody in the synagogue who heard the sermon was filled with wrath (read "madder 'n hell") and threw him out of the city and took him to its highest hill to throw him down to be stoned. Jesus had in effect said that in the final analysis God would not embrace holy mother church, or Israel, as the sole possessor of truth. What to them was blasphemy against the holy people was actually a prophetic challenge to their limited view of God. But corruption of consciousness still prevails two thousand years later, and *we* assume by static analogy that

Jesus in this sermon or Luke in this passage was rejecting Jews and accepting gentiles. In fact a number of biblical scholars today take this to be Luke's intention. But this is simply to ignore the truly prophetic dimension in much of what the Gospels report about Jesus' interpretation of Old Testament Scripture.

To get at Luke's answer to what happened at Nazareth we must ask *our*selves, "Why is it such an offense to have the man remind us that Elijah and Elisha did their works of grace to people outside the in-group?" Our own corruption of consciousness would have us believe we have moved beyond all that: of course we believe the church should give of its substance to the poor and dispossessed of the world.

But that is not what Jesus preached on this occasion. Jesus hit us with that once and for all when he quoted Deuteronomy 15 very plainly for all to hear—that we shall have the poor with us always: that is, there will always be the opportunity for us to be patronizing, to secure our liberal credentials by being benevolent. What Jesus was saying at Nazareth, and according to all the Gospels said with amazing frequency, was that Israel (the church, for us) ought to be that one institution in the world which lives, has its very existence, by and in the judgments of God (i.e., under the scrutiny of final truth). And that means knowing that final truth is simply not the possession of any one generation or any one in-group. And it means that we must rid ourselves of the idea that the church is the Society of the Saved. The primary message of the church is that *God* is God. The very purpose of its existence is to make that point clear. But, and God help us, the one institution in the world most in danger of domesticating God and reducing him to a partisan god of the in-group is the church (or temple, or synagogue, or mosque). To think that God is our God is to violate everything the Bible affirms: it is to subscribe to polytheism. I am convinced that twentieth-century man is as polytheistic as Iron Age man was; the only difference is that we do not recognize it. We call our polytheism monotheism—and that, according to prophetic realism, is the final falsehood. Jeremiah once said it was bad enough when the popular theologians of his day prophesied by the Canaanite deity Baal, but worse than that was their prophesying falsehood, that is, partisan truth, in the name of the one true God (Jer. 2:8; 6:30–31). For the church unabashedly to proclaim "God" when it means that great chairman of the board in the sky, is in the biblical view worse than communist atheism.

Paul Tillich, not long before his death, in speaking of the so-called death-of-god theologies remarked, "And now let us ask the church and all its members, including you and myself, a bold question. Could it be that in order to judge the misuse of his name within the church, God reveals himself from time to time by creating silence about himself? . . . Is the secular silence about God that we experience everywhere today perhaps God's way of forcing his church back to a scared embarrassment when speaking of him?"

And Jan Lochmann, the great Czech theologian, said in his inaugural speech at Union Seminary three years ago, "In Jesus Christ God did not become a Christian but a man: *ecce homo*."[*] We can all remember the slight shock we received as children to learn that God was not an Episcopalian, or a Presbyterian, or a Baptist, or a professor emeritus of Yale Divinity School. But I wonder if we have yet been shocked into the realization that God is not a Christian.

Jesus explained the explosive passage in Isaiah in a way totally unexpected and shocking by saying that the prophet of the eschaton, Elijah, will do in the end time what the Old Testament says he did originally: he will go outside the church.

The church today must by dynamic analogy try to hear Jesus' prophetic indiscretion at Nazareth.

Elijah's sustaining and being sustained by a Black Muslim, I mean a Phoenician widow, and Elisha's healing a commie, I mean a Syrian leper, is hard enough to take even when talking about the benevolence program of the church. But to suggest that in the final analysis God, our God, is the God of everybody else too, is entirely too much. We ask, like the folk at Nazareth, What's the use? And we do so because our normal view of hope and of truth *is* partisan. The church, which is charged with the message that

[*]Jan Lochmann, "The Church and the Humanization of Society," *Union Seminary Quarterly Review* 24 (1969): 138.

God is *God,* is the institution most in danger, precisely because of that mission, of domesticating God. In other words our normal churchly view of God is absolutely no better than the Ku Klux Klan view of God or the commie view of no-god—if anything is worse, as Jeremiah would say, because we claim for our partisan god the name of the one true God of all.

Jesus' sermon should reveal to us the secrets of *our* heart, *our* corruption of consciousness. As the author of the Epistle to the Hebrews put it, "Our judge is the God of all." He is not the cheer-leader of the in-group we as normal human beings have made him out to be. *God is one.* And God's radical oneness means for us the radical oneness of man. The Bible can be the church's indiscreet prophet if we read it right. And that means that in the Gospel lessons we must cease identifying with Jesus and identify rather with those who heard his words, that is, with the church of his day, so that we may be blessed by those judgments which alone can save and heal our own normal corruption of consciousness. The church is the earthen vessel in which the treasure of this message is conveyed: God is God and his oneness is ours.

I should like to try to match Paul Tillich's boldness by asking another question. Could it be that the way in which *we* may hear the voice of God in this age of the silence of God is by learning ways of hearing the voices of our enemies? Is this perhaps what the biblical tradition of God as the Stranger and Alien in our midst means for us today? And I don't mean our easy enemies. And I don't mean someone else's enemies. For some of us "enemy" means the Vietcong and for others of us it means John Mitchell. And I don't mean one's personal, petty enemies. I mean our real enemies, those we know in our heart of hearts are wrong. And I don't mean loving the doer and hating the deed—that is patron-izing to the extreme. Maybe it is when our rightness can hear their wrongness that we are hearing the voice of God. The central message of the Bible is not that man should believe in God. Maybe it isn't so important, you know, whether we do or not. The central message of the gospel is that God believes in man, and he came, it says, to affirm that belief. The radical oneness of God *is* the radical oneness of man. It is in order to proclaim that message that Israel, whether Judaism or Christianity or Islam, exists; and everything it does, every program it sponsors, must fall under the scrutiny of and be constantly challenged by that final truth.

It is abundantly clear that Christendom is dead; that is, the hope of Christianizing the world by Western imperialism has been exposed and recognized for the falsehood it was. In this sense the church, as Jeremiah and Jesus proclaimed, is going now into exile once more. It has again resumed its identity as a movement, a pilgrimage. Has not the time arrived under the guidance of God's Holy Spirit for the ecumenical movement to move on out beyond the Catholic-Protestant dialogue seriously to include conversation not only with Jews but also with Muslims, Buddhists, Communists, and even those odd sects cropping up all over? I do not mean conversations for cultic union, but humble efforts to hear what the hopes and fears of others are on this pitiful globe.

Perhaps we the church of Jesus Christ in abandoning the falsehood of the Christendom idea may now make a genuine pilgrimage into monotheistic pluralism. Would a pilgrimage into pluralism somehow dishonor Christ? No. I suggest on the contrary that the Christendom view of the church dishonored Christ and that the church's pilgrimage into pluralism, or what we might call Consciousness IV, would most honor the Christ who never pointed to himself but always pointed to the one God of all. And as Christian theology moves on out from the neoorthodoxy of the past fifty-two years and from its emphasis on Christocentric theology (or Christ-centered theology) it should embark on a pilgrimage into theocentric Christology (or God-centered Christianity)—a quest of the will of the one God of all mankind—not by claiming Christ but by truly *pro*claiming him and being released by him to perceive God's final truth in Creation and Incarnation.

What happened at Nazareth? Jesus interpreted Scripture, the life-giving tradition, as a challenge to our limited view of truth, and we tried to lynch him. Amen.

5. Banquet of the Dispossessed

"Banquet of the Dispossessed" was the first piece I sent to the USQR and the editors published it the spring before we moved from Rochester to New York where I assumed a position as professor of Old Testament (*USQR* 20 [1965]: 355-63). For the *USQR* I decontextualized the sermon to some extent and provided some footnotes to comfort those scholars who always seem to look for such, but it is stated there that I had preached the sermon in the Brick Church in Rochester, New York, on 31 August 1964.

Quite so. In a letter to the editors of the *USQR* dated 5 March 1965 I wrote: "It was a sermon originally preached in the Brick Presbyterian Church of Rochester on 31 August 1964, one month after the riots which rocked this city to its foundations. The form in which I submit it to you is essentially that of the original sermon, but I have added the three opening paragraphs and the footnotes."

I had for some time been working on the original first-century context in which Jesus told the parable of the Marriage Feast and Luke then wrote it up. I felt that some newly published Dead Sea Scroll fragments provided clues to what it was Jesus was challenging in the Lukan parable. The full scholarly presentation of my argument appeared later as "The Ethic of Election in Luke's Great Banquet Parable," in *Essays on Old Testament Ethics*, ed. J. L. Crenshaw and Willis Crenshaw (New York: Ktav Publishing House, 1974), pp. 247–71. I should perhaps also mention that the sermon in a revised form is available as "Invitation to the Dispossessed" through Thesis Theological Cassettes, vol. 4, no. 6 (1973).

But the following is from the original manuscript as preached in Rochester in August 1964, one month after the riots. Rochester was in a state of shock. Many prominent citizens who would normally not be in the city just before Labor Day were indeed in town, stunned. Some were scared. The boosters and positive thinkers were furious and the city was still smoldering. A colleague, William Hamilton, had some months earlier been vilified in the local press for suggesting that Rochester might have something to learn from the experience of

Birmingham, where he had attended the funeral of the four children who were killed by a bomb while sitting in church. At that point nobody was yet prepared to say Bill had been right, though he certainly had been. To admit that, however, might have been to accede to his recently published statements that God was dead.

Well, the old Rochester was not dead, only shaken. It was into that context that the following sermon was preached. I had to do it. To do anything less would have been unbearable. I had so far as I knew offended no one. But I knew that such a passage properly reviewed in the context of Rochester late summer 1964 had to be a challenge to the powerful and comfortable, if not offensive. At that point to comfort Rochesterians with power would have been unfaithful.

The hermeneutics of prophetic critique was explained at the beginning of the sermon. One of the basic aspects of that explanation was repeated in a different context in "The New History" (see chapter 2 above) where I also used the quotation from Peter Howard.

Psalm 146
Luke 14:7–24

As many of my friends in the Brick Church know, my profession is that of interpreter. I occupy the chair of Old Testament interpretation at the seminary and as such my main job is, like that of an interpreter at the United Nations, to translate ideas from one idiom into another. Most of my working hours currently are spent in translating and interpreting one of the Dead Sea Scrolls. The interpreter stands to one side in order to permit the speaker, whether ancient or modern, to make his point in the other language as clearly and as sharply as possible. But the interpreter utterly fails in his task if he translates only words. The interpreter must always translate idiomatically, carrying the intended sense from the one idiom to the other intact.

The Bible is not a product of modern times but of antiquity. Specifically, most of it comes from the Ancient Near East, and it is the job of the interpreter of the Bible to know the Ancient Near East, as well as the languages of the time, in order to adjudge correctly the impact and effect of the biblical statements upon those who *first* heard or read them. It is quite clear to the professionally trained biblical interpreter that Jesus was a daily embarrassment to the good, respectable religious people of his day, and it is equally clear that we in reading the New Testament today can miss the sense of that embarrassment unless we identify ourselves in the Gospel accounts *not* with Jesus but with those who were in his presence both blessed and discomfited by what he had to say.

His very first sermon, in Nazareth, was such an embarrassment; for the record of it in Luke 4 ends in what amounts to an attempt on the part of the good, respectable folk who heard the sermon to lynch Jesus because of what he had to say. He started his sermon with a stirring passage of Scripture from Isaiah 61 in which the prophet says that God's loving concern is for the poor of society, for prisoners, for the blind, and for the oppressed—that is, for the dispossessed. After reading the lesson from Isaiah, Jesus closed the scroll, handed it to the attendant, and said, "Today this scripture has been fulfilled in your hearing." How beautiful, they all said. They all spoke well of him and wondered at the gracious words at his command. He reads so well. Such comments remind one of God's consoling words to Ezekiel: "Your people who talk together about you by the walls and at the doors of the houses . . . come to you as people come, and they sit before you as my people, and they hear what you say but they will not do it; for with their lips they show much love, but their heart is set on their gain. And, lo, you are to them like one who sings love songs with a beautiful voice and plays well on an instrument, for they hear what you say, but they will not do it" (Ezek. 33:30–32). Thus it was with the good people in Nazareth who heard Jesus: "Is not this Joseph's son?" As though fearful however that his neighbors had misunderstood him, Jesus stressed the prophetic or offensive aspect of his sermon by recalling acts of grace performed by the popular ancient prophets Elijah and Elisha. Though there were in his day many widows in Israel, Elijah was sent to none of them but instead to a foreigner, the Sidonian widow Zarephath, to help her, and though there were many lepers in Israel in his day, Elisha cleansed only a foreigner, the Syrian Naaman.

At that point Jesus' hearers got his message, "and all in the synagogue were filled with wrath. And they rose up and put him out f the city, and led him to the brow of the hill on which their city vas built, that they might throw him down headlong." The transator or interpreter of such a passage is obligated to attempt to onvey to the modern reader and hearer the reaction of our anient counterparts who that day actually heard Jesus himself. Iow can we translate for ourselves the great offense in what Jesus aid in order to understand why his friends, neighbors, and ousins in Nazareth wanted to lynch him? Before he had made lear his own understanding of the passage from Isaiah the same eople had thought his words gracious, perhaps even inspired. 3ut when he exegeted or interpreted for them what he felt the rophets themselves had in mind they reacted with violence.

The power of the gospel judges us and saves us not by our dentifying with Jesus in the lynching scene but by our identifyng with the lynchers, by knowing that if we had been in that ynagogue that day and heard him preach that sermon we should ave been highly offended at him ourselves. Maybe we would not e quite so violent as to join a lynching party, for no one pictures imself willingly as an extremist. Perhaps we would simply want o write the preacher a note and warn him that by saying such hings he was stirring up the poor people and giving them hopes hey should not have. At any rate we do not succeed in lynching esus that day, although we do succeed in doing so on a dark 'riday a bit later on. Of course what really offended Jesus' hearers o much in that first sermon was his citing the biblical truth of 3od's loving concern for foreigners. What really angered the ;ood, positive-thinking churchgoers that day was his citing of Clijah's and Elisha's acts of grace toward the Sidonian widow nd the Syrian leper. Translated that means, if we can catch the ffense of it accurately, that Jesus told his hearers that God loves hose whom we mistrust and speaks through them to us.

Rabbi Marc H. Tanenbaum said recently that at the root of our acial problem is the "failure of the majority of the white American people to begin to comprehend the magnitude of the tragedy f the Negro in America. The capture and forcible migration of nillions of Negroes from Africa to this country between the ixteenth and nineteenth centuries was a crime which has never een equaled in size and intensity and is perhaps comparable only

to the persecutions of our own times under the Nazis. The onl
analogy I can think of," said the rabbi, "is the reaction of the Jew
of today who reads of what happened to his forebears in Western
Christendom—the chain of persecutions, pogroms, expulsions
autos-da-fé, and finally genocide."*

Can a rabbi teach us of the love of Christ? Or can a Britishe
teach us of the strength of America?

Peter Howard, the British author and playwright, said in an
address given in Atlanta last winter: "The different races in
America are her strength and glory. They are an asset no othe
country possesses. . . . My faith," he continued, "is in modern
America. I believe Americans will arise with a character tha
convicts, captivates, and changes nations. I believe those who
have suffered most will show the greatest passion and compas
sion for long-suffering humanity. I believe those who have been
victims of the worst discrimination will be the first to heal the
hates and fears of others because they themselves are free from
fear and hate. I am convinced men and women who for genera
tions have drunk the water of tears and eaten the bread of
bitterness will give living water and the bread of life to millions
trembling, longing, hoping, waiting, praying for the new type of
man and the new type of society that will lead the world into
lasting justice, liberty, and peace. Those who have passed through
the fires of persecution can hold forth one hand to persecutor
and persecuted alike, and with the other uplift a flame of free
dom to illuminate the earth. . . . It remains my belief," he said
"that crossless Christians do more to camouflage the reality of
Christ's revolution for humanity than any Communist or Fascist."

The Bible says many times throughout both the Old and the
New Testaments that God's most tender concern is for the dis
possessed. The thrust of the whole biblical story of God's loving
desire for people is from divinity to humanity, from majesty to
humility. God's majesty in the Bible is defined and described no
in terms of how splendid he is in the company of the gods on Mt
Zaphon or on Mt. Olympus but in terms of his condescension

*Marc H. Tanenbaum, *New York Times,* 23 August 1964, p. 10.
†Peter Howard, *New York Times,* 29 March 1964, p. 10E.

his stooping to have fellowship not with gods but with man. Divine majesty in the Bible is from the human point of view abject humility. The Bible says that God chose a motley crew of slaves in Egypt to be his special people and chose a humble stable in Bethlehem in which to express his final humility, his total love, his holy will to be born a man. And our Lord time and again attempted in his parables and in his teaching generally to remind his contemporaries of the majesty of God's humility and of how they, that is to say we, should emulate his humility, or as the prophet Micah stressed, how we should walk humbly with God because God has walked humbly with us.

And I think that we can nowhere better perceive our Lord's lesson for us in this regard than in his teaching on the etiquette of banquets in Luke 14. Jesus had been invited to dinner on a Sabbath. It was in the home of a rich Pharisee, and Jesus noted how those invited coveted the places of honor at table, the places near the host at the head of the table. He pointed out to them a simple observation: those who try to claim a seat of honor, that is, exalt themselves, will be in danger of being asked by the host to sit further down; and those who instead choose a lowly seat, that is, humble themselves, may be asked by the host to go up higher.

And then Jesus gave the host a lesson in Amy Vanderbilt or Emily Post. "He said also to the man who had invited him, 'When you give a dinner or a banquet, do not invite your friends or your brothers or your kinsmen or rich neighbors, lest they also invite you in return and you be repaid.'" Quite clearly those were precisely the people present with Jesus at the table. Again we must identify with the rich Pharisee to get the power of the judgment of Jesus' lesson. Jesus is saying, do not invite just those of your own station and status. As he clearly says in the Sermon on the Mount, if you love only those who love you, what reward have you? And then he continued, "But when you give a feast, invite the poor, the maimed, the lame, the blind, and you will be blessed because they cannot repay you." Now let's see if we can translate the offense of it. But when you give a feast, invite the riffraff, the beggars, the ugly, those who do not pull themselves up by their own bootstraps, those who seemingly refuse to better themselves because they are lazy, trifling, and undeserving. Mind you, here we sit at a fine banquet, honored guests of a fine leader of the community, and this Galilean teacher says we should fraternize with the very people who are a blight on our fine city, who live in and yes cause those slums which give our community such a bad name. You sell them a decent house and in two years it'll be run down and cancerous to the neighborhood around it. And this Galilean wants us to socialize with them.

The job of translating a biblical text is at best a difficult one, and the hardest task is finding the right analogy so as to bring out the offensive judgment of God which alone saves and redeems. One hermeneutic or interpretation rule that one can always with confidence follow is the one that stresses that whenever our reading of a biblical passage makes us feel self-righteous we can be sure that we have misread it; and the concomitant rule is that whenever our reading of a biblical passage brings home to us the poignant judgment and salvation of God's humility we can be sure we have read it correctly.

Another such rule of biblical interpretation is one which says we should always avail ourselves of as many pertinent nonbiblical texts from the Bronze, Iron, Persian, Early Jewish, Hellenistic, and Roman periods as will help to understand the text and to ask the right questions which will unlock the meaning of the passage addressed. In the case of the next paragraph in Luke 14 we have from the so-called Dead Sea Scrolls just such a passage. It is from the Essene or Qumran Rule of the Congregation, and it deals specifically with those who may be invited to the Essene congregation and with the seating arrangement at the Essene messianic banquet (1 QSa II, 5–22).

After specifying that "anyone afflicted in his flesh, crippled of feet or hands, lame or blind or deaf or dumb . . . of poor eyesight or senility" is not to be admitted to the congregation of the men of renown, the Essene Rule proceeds to give the seating arrangement of the men of renown who are invited to the great banquet when the Messiah comes. It is carefully laid down that the high priest is to sit at the head of the banquet table, then the elders of the priests, then the heads of the divisions of Israel, then the heads of the elders of the congregation and the scribes. In each category the phrase "each according to his status" is used.

Then when they have all been seated "each according to his status" to eat the bread and drink the wine of the messianic banquet (on which our own Holy Communion is based) the high priest blesses the first bite of bread and the cup of wine. After him the Messiah may take bread and then the assembled congregation. It is of course the most exclusive kind of closed communion, and the reason given for excluding the poor and the lame is that they might offend the holy angels (and God himself, one might assume).

Now mind you, back at the table in the rich ruler's house Jesus had just told the host that he would be blessed if he invited not such men of renown, his social equals, but the slum dwellers. Some good student of the Law on hearing Jesus say this ventured a suggestion which would put the conversation on quite a different level, and he countered Jesus' saying with the orthodox Essene and Pharisaic belief, "Blessed is he who shall eat bread in the kingdom of God!" In other words his retort to Jesus was that true blessedness will come in the beyond, at the eschaton, to the acceptable men of renown and status. The implication in the remark was clearly that the truly faithful, the Pharisees and perhaps the Essenes who kept themselves pure and undefiled, would be the ones invited to the messianic banquet, the men of renown. Jesus had obviously shocked his hearers by listing as invitees the very ones shut out and forbidden by the Essene Rule of the Congregation and by Pharisaic Oral Law.

And now in response to this attempt to put him in his place Jesus compounds the offense by telling a parable to the assembled company at the rich man's table. "A man once gave a great banquet and invited many; and at the time for the banquet he sent his servant to say to those who had been invited, 'Come, for all is ready.'" Jesus takes the bull by the horns and prepares in a parable to deal precisely with the proper list of acceptable invitees. "But they all alike began to make excuses." We are all familiar with the excuses: one of the invitees had just bought a field and could not come, another had bought a yoke of oxen and could not come, and another had just gotten married and could not come. And here is one of the many points in the Bible where it is absolutely necessary to know the biblical and contemporary context. One cannot possibly go from one's own twentieth-century existentialist experience straight to this text and read there what Jesus is trying to say: one must as always know the biblical, that is, Old Testament, and contemporary Early Jewish context of the passage. The excuses which are offered by the invitees in Jesus' parable are taken from the list of excuses or exemptions listed in Deuteronomy 20 for those who are to be excluded from the ranks of the faithful who are to fight in the great holy war. And these are the same exemptions listed in Mishnah Sotah (M. Sotah VIII) in the Talmud and in the Dead Sea War Scroll (1 QM X, 5) from Qumran, of those who are to be excluded from the ranks of the faithful who with holy angels are to engage in the great and final messianic battle against the forces of darkness and evil. It is important to know that the messianic banquet and the messianic battle are seen as two parts of the same eschatological event. It is as though Jesus had a copy of the Talmud tradition in one hand and a copy of the Essene rule in the other and purposefully set out to deny them both. We can at least be quite sure that Jesus knew both the Pharisaic and the Essene doctrines of the eschaton. He has just been challenged by one of the honored guests at table with him concerning who would be invited to the messianic banquet, and Jesus responds that even at that table one will find the same riffraff he has just recommended the host should invite to be truly blessed.

The Essene War Scroll (1 QM VII, 4–5), like the Rule of the Congregation, specifically excludes those Jesus says will be there. "Any one halt or blind or lame, or a man in whose body is a permanent defect, or a man affected by an impurity of his flesh, all these shall not go forth to battle with them [i.e., with the faithful and the angels]." In utter contrast Jesus in the parable continues, "Then the householder in wrath said to his servant, 'Go out quickly to the streets and lanes of the city, and bring in the poor and maimed and blind and lame.'" The householder, according to Jesus, ends by saying, "For I tell you, none of those men who were invited shall taste my banquet."

Jesus thereby sharply and completely rejected the implication that the pure and undefiled Pharisees and Essenes would alone be present at the great messianic banquet. On the contrary he denies that any such will be present but that the guests at that table will bear a striking resemblance to the original Israel, the refugee slaves from Africa, Egypt, who at Sinai ate bread and drank wine in God's awful presence at the foot of the mountain. Far from its being an exclusive table of society's finest, those who eat bread in the kingdom of God will on the contrary be the dispossessed, the undeserving, the rabble, the riffraff; and far from the seating at that table being in any way limited, the servant tells the master, "Sir, what you commanded has been done, and still there is room."

There is always a place at God's table and in his kingdom for the dispossessed, for him who can say, "I am undeserving of an invitation, I can make no claim on him, I am unworthy so much as to gather up the crumbs under that table, and my name does not appear on the list of the pure and undefiled." It is to the person who knows the judgment of God on his life and who knows he cannot so much as measure up to God's humility in Christ, much less his majesty, that salvation and redemption come. In other words not until we modern Essenes and Pharisees, we Presbyterians and Baptists, cease to view the dispossessed as riffraff but rather as our brothers in the kingdom of God, not until we know that we like them can make no claim on God will we have experienced the judgment of the gospel which redeems and saves. Not until Jesus offends us by his rabble-rousing teaching and we admit that if we had been there we like the Pharisees and Essenes would have jailed him and tried him and crucified him, not until we know the judgment of God's grace of forgiveness for having crucified him can we be transformed, redeemed, and saved. When the dispossessed have ceased to be "they" and "them" and have become "we" and "us," when we realize that we like them have no claim to make, no status to defend, and no place of honor to boast, then shall we know the power of the good news that still there is room. When we have ceased to talk about how to "make them behave" and can start asking how we all should behave, and when we have fully realized that our Lord, and the God in him, was himself counted among the dispossessed, then perhaps we shall know the blessing of unrequited grace.

"And the servant said, 'Sir, what you commanded has been done, and still there is room.'"

PART TWO

THE PASSION OF THE
GOD OF POWER

6. In the Same Night...

A few of the elements toward the end of "In the Same Night . . ." had been part of my thinking about the power of the cross as early as the closing pages of my *Old Testament in the Cross* (New York: Harper & Row, Publishers, 1961). But the basic concept of the sermon developed out of the agonies of the Vietnam War. It was written specifically for delivery in James Chapel at Union Seminary on the first Vietnam moratorium day, 15 October 1969 (and subsequently published in *USQR* 25 [1970]: 333–41).

The nation was in turmoil. The Columbia Bust and Free University had taken place a year and a half earlier, and Richard Nixon had been elected president (largely due to the rigid purity of the students in refusing to work for Hubert Humphrey) just a year before. The war was expanding on the argument that the United States had to send more troops to protect the troops already there. Draft cards were being burnt: the air was full of violence. Very few people suggested seeing more than one side to an issue. Those were the days when one was either a part of the solution or a part of the problem. Singularism was the order of the day. Many academic people viewed calm reflection as a cop-out. In some quarters authority derived wholly from having been in a march and faced nightsticks, dogs, or hoses.

Union Seminary was being dismantled bit by bit. Most of the students had fairly clear visions of evil but little constructive vision for improvement. As Saul Alinsky said when speaking on campus that fall, "Some of these students burn like pure, blue flames of fire." They were so frustrated by their attempt to fight evil in society that they rebelled against their foster mothers the academic institutions. Union had embarked on a new system of governance centering in the Union Assembly, made up of all the faculty and half again as many students elected among themselves. Unfortunately the students had very little guidance or help from the faculty. A few faculty members surfaced as skillful brokers of student power but most of us abdicated responsibility in utter confusion. None of us had any training in how to be responsible in such a situation. I fear we failed Union in those crucial days. Most of the institutional changes made then have since been rescinded; the few that remain are superficial. Unfortunately the ethos completely changed. The Union I knew when I went there in 1965, and to which I brought my dream for a center for biblical studies, got lost in the fray. The abiding result of all that furor is that whereas in the mid-1960s excellence was expected and sponsored, in 1969 one had to apologize for engaging in apparently irrelevant scholarship: the pressures are still largely for immediate relevance, not for enduring excellence. Some colleagues do not agree with this assessment.

"In the Same Night . . ." is a communion sermon, a celebration of the theologem *errore hominum providentia divina*: God's grace works in and through human sinfulness. The hermeneutic is that of prophetic critique: Christ cannot be identified with any one side of our conflicts, but came and got crushed *between* the zealots and the establishment. One of the techniques of activists in those days was to intimidate those who might disagree with them by trying to make them feel somehow sub-Christian. We can see ourselves in the sins and foibles of those portrayed in the Passion account, especially in the disciples about the table; but Christ's hand is that of the stranger, offering us himself.

The tradition which Paul reports in 1 Corinthians 11 was possibly a nucleus of a Christian *haggadah*. In the Jewish Passover meal, or Seder, the youngest at table able to do so asks the question "How is this night different from all others?" The head of the household then answers by telling the story of redemption. It is a cue to tell the biblical Torah story. So it is just possible that the story which begins, "In the same night that he was betrayed, he took bread . . ." was the core of a Christian adaptation of the Passover *haggadah*. Like the *haggadah* the Eucharist or Holy Communion is based on the ancient concept of memory, or *anamnēsis*, in which the ancient story is represented, brought into the present moment with the participants taking the ancient roles. Time and space, those immense guarantors of human limitation, are transcended, and by memory, or in remembrance of him, the church is one: all the millions through the centuries and around the world are caught up in the twelve about the table.

God's grace comes to us even in our folly, indeed came to us even in the tragedy and folly of the late 1960s, judging and by faith redeeming.

Luke 22:14–24
1 Corinthians 11:23–28

In 1 Corinthians 11:23 Paul provides us with the tradition which has become the words of institution for celebration of Holy Communion. But for many of us the words are perhaps too familiar. We have heard them so often they have become like a cue line from a prompter to begin a periodic drama of the church which has for the most part lost its meaning because we no longer find our identity in it.

Even within these walls one suspects that only so-called experts pay close attention to the verse; for in it are imbedded two of the thorniest and yet most exciting problems of New Testament scholarship: the mode of Paul's reception of this tradition "from the Lord," and the calendar problem about on which night this gathering in the upper room and the subsequent arrest and trials took place. Either problem alone could absorb the lifetime and constitute the vocation of a first-rate scholar; and they are both signaled in this one verse.

But I want us to think theologically about the juxtaposition of the time reported in the tradition with the scene which it depicts. "In the same night that he was betrayed he took bread . . ." It was on the night in which we betrayed him that he broke the bread and gave it to us. No matter what decision we make about the calendar and no matter how Paul received the tradition, we know that God expresses his grace in the midst of our sin: we know that God comes to us in our betrayal of him. This is both a prior knowledge and an existential knowing.

It is a prior knowledge because the Old Testament tells us that is the way God is. A wandering, perishing Aramaean was our father when God chose him. Oppressed slaves in Egypt were our fathers when God said to Moses, "Go tell them I'll be there." We already know about this God in the canon we recite when we "remember him." The word *remembrance* (Hebrew *zikkaron*, Greek *anamnēsis*) signals an act of worship. It means we tell

again the old, old story about how God acts, and when we do so
we identify not with God but with our fathers. And thus do we
know that in our father Abraham we lied about Sarah to save
our own skin. And thus do we know that in Jacob we deceived our
father Isaac to procure his blessing. And thus do we know that
we sold our brother Joseph into slavery because he offended us
with his dreams. And thus do we know that though God saved
us from slavery to Egypt, we rebelled against the freedom he
gave. And thus do we know that we have defiled every gift he has
given us by seeking our identity in those gifts instead of in the
embrace of the Giver. And thus do we know that in the same night
we betrayed him he took bread. It is a prior knowledge.

But it is also an existential knowing. For that was our night,
our big moment to be all that we should have been. We live that
night through again and again. We know it well, and the remarkable thing is that there is nothing evil in how we live that night.
On the contrary everything we do all that night long is normal
and understandable. Our father Abraham lied for the very existential reason that if he had told the truth he would have been
killed. Jacob deceived his father precisely because he coveted his
blessing. And our selling the intolerable Joseph into slavery was
clearly not as bad as killing him, which was apparently the alternative solution for one as obnoxious as Joseph had been. We
should always keep in mind that in our act of remembrance, that
is, in identifying in the biblical story with our origins, we do so
not to browbeat ourselves or to effect some soul purging by
sniveling about how wretched we are but rather to realize that
they back there were no better or worse than we today. The solutions they sought to their problems of *Existenz* are much the same
as our solutions today. Ramses, Nebuchadnezzar, Herod, and Pilate were not evil personified but on the contrary represented the
responsible world powers of their time in which we see our own
most responsible efforts well reflected. The power of the gospel
story in both the Old and the New Testaments strikes us and
becomes available to us not when we identify with Joseph, Jeremiah, and Christ but when we see ourselves in those about them.

Everything we do all that night long is normal and understandable—until the force of the next phrase strikes us: "he took bread

. . ." And then it is that somehow we can't quite bear ourselves. Our excuses and defenses and deceits are shattered. The defensible and normal become offensive and shameful. He took bread on the same night we betrayed him.

That was our night, the night the church was conceived. And we were all there, all twelve of us, seated about the table. Let us therefore in *anamnēsis* reassemble in the upper room both to sit at the table and to look at ourselves. It will be traumatic, but if we are not ready to come as we are and to see ourselves as we are, then we should not come. For to shy away from seeing ourselves as we really are is to confess that we have no place at that table: we deny that we are a part of that conception, we admit that we have not been born into the church. We are all there, all twelve of us. By the cultic principle of remembrance both time and space regain a mythic dimension. In the eschaton, or, in the idiom of the writer of the Epistle to the Hebrews, at that moment when the pilgrim church is about to cross the threshold over into the city of the living God, then, at that moment, the whole church is present—all the generations of the past, the dead whom we mourn, as well as all those alive today no matter where they are. In the celebration of the Holy Communion the whole church is present and the barriers of both time and space have been transcended; for it is in the celebration of the Holy Communion that the church is eschatologized. Wherever and whenever this celebration takes place the church for that moment is the pilgrim church arriving, just about to step over the threshold. And it is in this act of remembrance that the whole church is present or, again as Hebrews would say, we are surrounded by "so great a cloud of witnesses" (Heb. 12:1).

Let us take our places then about the table. In Luke 22 we read, "Then Satan entered into Judas Iscariot, who was of the number of the twelve." The shock is too much. Why must we look first at Judas? And yet I know of a certainty that because Judas was there I am not excluded. What if he had not been present? Then that bread would not be for me. I, Judas the betrayer, am at the table and receive the bread and the cup. If he had excluded me then I would have known for certain that I had done right in opting out. And it is not because I am so horrible; nor was Judas, the political activist, so horrible. But there it is, the bread from his own hand he bids me eat. In the same night that I betrayed him he took bread and blessed it and broke it and gave it to me.

But we don't know who it is our Lord means when he says the betrayer is at table with him. So the text says we began to wonder who it was that would do such a thing. And then the most normal thing happened: we all started bickering (Luke 22:23–24). Normal because when we protest our innocence we point to our credentials. How could it be I? we hear ourselves ask. I was with him in Galilee; I was right there at Caesarea Philippi; I went out with the seventy. So we started the discussion about who would be the greatest in the kingdom. Look at my record, we say. We forget the word of judgment and start reviewing our credentials. The picture of the church grows clearer; the picture of the Union Seminary community grows clearer. And we don't stop our bickering about which image or structure of the seminary is the correct one until our Lord breaks in and assures us that each of us will have a throne and be a servant (Luke 22:25–30).

And then he turns to Peter and says to us, "Simon, Satan wants you but I have prayed for you. You will deny me this night, all night you will deny that you know me—right up to dawn itself." And he looks deep into our eyes, as he will later on from the balcony; and we make our feeble vows of fidelity: "To prison and to death" I'll go (Luke 22:33).

Then knowing the stuff we're made of he tells us to bring along our money-bags and our swords and accompany him to the garden. How he knows us better than we know ourselves! We must have our money and swords; for these are our crutches, these are our ego. These protect us from ourselves. They build our ego and we need them lest we face the awful truth of who we are.

But we don't use them yet awhile. We go with him into the garden and he bids us watch and pray while he goes off alone himself to pray. He asks us to be men for him as he goes himself into the totality of loneliness to experience the agony of being a man. "Remove this cup from me" (Luke 22:42); and he perspired drops of blood. If there is a blood atonement surely this is it: Jesus experiencing the agony of being human, fully and completely and totally. I am a man. Oh, God, I don't seek suffering and death. I don't want to die.

His loneliness is but accentuated when he returns to find us asleep. He asked us to be men for him, a man, and we all fall asleep. The picture of the church becomes clearer.

And then it happened. The soldiers and the priests and Judas came. And Judas kissed him. Then our ire is up, our indignation kindled, and we rise to the occasion. "Lord, shall we strike with the sword?" (Luke 22:49). And one of us strikes a slave of the high priest and cuts off his ear. We wake up from our lethargy. Indignant and self-righteous we gather our forces, we muster our strength and go forth to the fray. We set out on our crusade: we nick a little piece of an ear. What awful reality is this in the Passion account that we must see ourselves for what we are? Jesus says to the crowd, "This is your hour" (Luke 22:53). And we all flee, every one of us abandons him—with our purses and with our swords.

Then Peter. With Peter we deny we ever knew him. All our vows are of no avail. We never really knew him. Yes, right there in the court we confess it to the woman: we never really knew him (Luke 22:57). And in that lie we finally told the truth.

And then with the rays of dawn he looks at us from the balcony. The text says, "The Lord turned and looked at Peter." Each of us must decide for himself what it was Peter saw in those eyes. What a comfort it would be if we could convince ourselves that in them we heard the reprimand You see, Peter, I told you so. But no, I fear we all know what it was we saw there: Peter, I do love you still. And with Peter we go out and weep bitterly.

And that was the night he broke bread with us. But the picture means nothing until we accept that bread and that cup. For we have no place in the picture unless we accept him. He offers himself through the din of our betrayals and bickering and feeble vows and lethargy and folly and denials. Through it all his hand proffers the broken bread. Take, eat, broken for you. In the same night that he was betrayed he took bread—and begot us, the church. And with Job who lamented the night of his conception we cry out, "That night—let thick darkness seize it! Let it not rejoice among the days of the year, let it not come into the number of the months. Yea, let that night be barren; let no joyful cry be heard in it. Let those curse it who curse the day, who are skilled to rouse up Leviathan. Let the stars of its dawn be dark;

let it hope for light, but have none, nor see the eyelids of the morning" (Job 3:6–9). But my Lord! What a morning when the Lord turned and looked at Peter! "My Lord, what a morning when the stars begin to fall," says the jubilee song. For it is in this act of remembrance, it is in this moment of the ongoing church eschatologized in Holy Communion with its Lord that we know of a certainty that he *is* Lord whether the morning stars sing together (Job 38:7) or the stars begin to fall (Joel 2:10).

For it is in this Holy Communion with him that we know that in Christ God judges us at our best. The power of the gospel strikes us not in our "total depravity" but in our best efforts to be responsible, obedient, good, and effective. Judas' worst fault was that he took the advice of the church leaders of his day and for services rendered received an honorarium. The church leaders' worst fault was an effort to save the church and state of their day from political and physical disaster at the hands of the Roman legions. Peter's worst fault in his denying his Lord was that he had followed him to his trial, whereas the others had not. Pilate's worst fault was in abstaining from making a decision he rightly felt incompetent to make. The Roman soldiers' worst fault was in their obedience to the orders to which they were assigned. And in them all we see ourselves, and we know that we too put him there. Is it depravity to follow the advice of our priests and bishops? Is it depravity to want a more activist, political leader? Is it depravity for priests and bishops and magistrates to try to maintain law and order? Is it depravity to follow our Lord in his trials though we cannot join him on the cross? Is it wrong to abstain from judgment? Is it wrong to be obedient? Each of us knows experientially and personally the life situation of those who crucified our Lord.

With Johann Hermann we ask and answer the question:

> Who was the guilty? Who brought this upon thee?
> Alas, my treason, Jesus, hath undone thee!
> 'Twas I, Lord Jesus, I it was denied thee;
> I crucified thee.

Like them we have our own excuses, our visions of a better society, and our own special cases which we plead in defense. But then we are confronted by the broken body on the cross.

And we know that our excuses are nothing. The brief wherewith we would defend ourselves crumbles like dust in our pleading hands. We witness all our goodness and righteousness shattered in the shocking sight before us.

And with Isaiah (64:6) we confess,

> We have all become like one who is unclean,
> And all our righteous deeds are like a filthy rag.

It is because we know these things, it is because we believe that in the night of man's folly when he is apparently at his worst, killing and being killed because of ideological chalk lines and hating and being hated because of political affiliations, when mankind's blindness and stupidity and fear are apparently at their worst, *he* comes and breaks bread and gets himself crushed between the zealots and the establishment for our sake: "This is my body which is broken for you."

No excuse or defense we can proffer could possibly increase the love which there surrounds us or the forgiveness which there indicts us. And then we realize in our existential knowing that salvation is also judgment, a judgment more trenchant than any of which our prior knowledge from the Old Testament speaks, the judgment of his grace: I do love you still.

In the same night, the tradition says, in the same night . . . Amen.

Prayers for the Dead

To remember in biblical usage often means quite simply to worship, to engage in a cultic act of worship which centers in a recitation of the biblical story. It is the recitation of the story, or reading of the canon, which legitimizes or authorizes the worship service; for remembrance means, first and foremost, remembering God's grace, his acts of grace toward us, his people.

But remembrance has also another and closely related meaning, for it also means calling to the mind of God our own condition. In petitionary and intercessory prayers, as opposed to prayers of praise and thanksgiving, we remind God or bring into his presence our concerns, our hopes and fears for ourselves and for others.

And then there is a very special connotation of remembrance subsumed under this second meaning to which I wish to draw our attention today. And that is the remembrance of the dead. Not only does remembrance of the dead mean a prayer that God remember the souls of those who have departed, it also means that the church militant and the church triumphant are one church precisely when the Holy Communion instituted by our Lord is celebrated, as he commanded us, "in remembrance" of him. The whole church is present in the celebration, those alive and those departed, so that when we take the bread and the cup we know that we are surrounded by a great cloud of witnesses.

It is in this sense of the word *memorial*, or *remembrance*, that I wish while the present assembled community is gathered in prayer to name the names of some of those in the *nephos marturon* (cloud of witnesses) which surrounds us (Hebrews 12:1). Let us pray:

For the nearly seven hundred thousand northern and southern Vietnamese and American soldiers who have died in Vietnam and the larger number of civilians whose numbers are not known. In lieu of reading all their names, which would be impossible here, I name the name of Russell Flesher, a Union Seminary student who two years ago was killed in action there.

For the numerous Americans, black and white, who have died in America in the cause of civil rights and civil liberties. In naming the names of a few we remember before God all those who have died that this country may know true freedom and true justice for all its citizens:

Emmett Till	James Cheyney
The four children killed in the bombing of the 16th Street Baptist Church of Birmingham	Andrew Goodman
	James Reeb
	Viola Liuzzo
	Medgar Evers
John Kennedy	Martin Luther King, Jr.
Michael Schwerner	Robert Kennedy

For those of the Union Seminary community who have died in the past year. Two of these, Richard Harper and James Tallis, both of the Music School, died in youth. Seven of those who have died in the past year lived their lives to full maturity. These were men and a woman who helped to shape this seminary into the community it is today. They fought their battles in their day and fought them well:

Mrs. Edmund Steimle	Paul Scherer
Charles Iglehart	Russell Bowie
Daniel Fleming	Harry Emerson Fosdick
Clarence Dickinson	

Mindful of the presence of the saints and martyrs, the great and the lowly, the named and the nameless, and of the whole family of man whether they be Christian, Muslim, Jewish, Buddhist, or Communist, all of God's children in Vietnam and in this country, I ask you to rise and recite with me the Mourners' Qaddish, one of the most ancient affirmations of faith known amongst the peoples of God:

> Magnified and sanctified be God's great name in this world which he has created according to his will. May his kingdom come in your lifetime and in your days and in the lifetime of the whole household of faith, speedily and very soon.
> And say ye: Amen.
>
> May his great name be blessed forever and ever and ever. Blessed, praised, glorified, exalted, extolled, honored, magnified, and lauded be the name of the Holy One blessed be he, even he who is above every blessing, every song, every praise, and every consolation which man might utter.
> And say ye: Amen.
>
> May the name of the Lord be blessed from henceforth even forevermore. May abundant peace from heaven and life rain down upon us and upon all the household of faith.
> And say ye: Amen.
>
> May he who makes peace in his lofty heights make peace upon us and upon all the world.
> And say ye: Amen.

7. Outside the Camp

"Outside the Camp" was first preached at Battell Chapel of Yale University on 6 October 1968 (and published in *USQR* 24 [1969]: 239–46). President Kingman Brewster took part in the service and Chaplain William Sloane Coffin, Jr., administered Communion.

Most of us in the academic world were in a state of shock that fall as classes resumed in more or less traditional shells on campuses that had been rocked to the foundations the spring before. Changes were being effected. At Union, Dr. Lloyd Bailey and I stayed in New York most of the summer revamping the introductory Old Testament course for the fall. The message we had received from the students in 1967 and again during the Columbia Bust and Free University of the spring of 1968 was that we should humanize the educational process and try to relate to the students on as nearly a one-to-one basis as possible. We reduced the number of "faculty monologues," the students' term for lectures, and greatly increased participation in the preceptorial groups. And taking a cue from a practice I had instigated in Rochester, Bailey and I handpicked a group of upperclasspersons in the B.D. (now M.Div.) program who had done well in Old Testament and who were also popular with other students, in some instances were even leaders of the student movement for change. These we gave the name *Ḥabiru* (a Bronze Age term for migrant workers and the same Semitic root as that of the word *Hebrew*). They participated with tutors and faculty in the preceptorials and made themselves available to answer student questions only they were in a position to answer; they formed, then and for several years thereafter, a valuable bridge between the tutors (already being identified with faculty) and the younger students. Much of this and more is described in the language of the time in "Teaching and Learning: The Old Testament at Union," *The Tower* (Union Theological Seminary, Fall 1968): 3–5.

The tenor of the time could be felt in a conversation in my office that fall. It was office hour just after a lecture in which I had invested a great deal of time and effort. I had returned to my office feeling deeply that I was responding to the students and being responsible to them. The student came in, sat down, and calmly said that the lecture was terrible (his very word). I asked him to explain. He replied that I should not begin Old Testament study with Moses. Immediately I felt that here was a student I could relate to, someone who had been reading Albright perhaps, who disagreed with the Germans and felt that that particular lecture should have begun with Abraham. Far from it. No way. The next words out of his mouth left me speechless: "You should begin with me!"

That conversation was in mind when I wrote "Outside the Camp." We were indeed present in the events the Bible records, if read by certain hermeneutics, but not in ways the student had in mind. This sermon was in large measure intended as an antidote to the egoism rampant in the students of the time, and especially their self-righteousness in feeling that their generation was exceptionally moral and ethical and imbued with visions no one else had ever had. It was quite clear that their basic protests against government policy in the Vietnam War and against the racism in society were shared across many lines by most thinking people, and the sermon recognizes that. But their delusions of purity deriving from attempting to sever their identity from the past in stressing that they were the *now* generation was Ezekiel 18 read totally out of context and a shock to my whole system. Students taught me much in those days and helped me review presuppositions of many sorts, but their view of their authority was both evil and false. Someone had to speak up.

The Bible does "start with us," after God, in Adam and Eve. There are many clear mirrors for our identity, for seeing who we are in the Bible. To heed the call to go "outside the camp" is not a vocation to create a generation of deluded purists but to fulfill a role God can weave into his plans and purposes, sinful though we may be. That is to monotheize. To fail to monotheize is to play—as many of the brightest students did—into the hands of those who saw in the student bursts of energy an opportunity they themselves would not otherwise have.

"Outside the Camp" was a cry to theologize, more specifically to monotheize, to try to view the apparent chaos of the times as a redemptive judgment of God but to view *all of us* in it as under that judgment and to view God as nonpartisan, getting crushed between the zealots and the establishment, thus judging both to the core, stripping both completely naked. The context of the fall of 1968 needed, I felt, the blazing light of the Crucified One judging us all and exposing equally the sham in us all. I left the scene there as the end of the sermon indicates: he just keeps on hanging there. I drew no moral nor suggested how anyone should react to the exposure. Some apparently missed the point entirely. Bill Coffin's one comment after the service was about the language used.

Much of the shock of the whole period of 1968 to 1974 has worn off, but not the horror of seeing many bright students feeling so self-righteous that they were convinced judgment fell only on others, nor the dread at seeing a few faculty members manipulate the students to their own agendas. One felt powerless. To say anything of the sort directly would have invited vilification; and I was so vilified on occasion and rendered ineffective. My own worst experience of the whole period was to come the following late February and March when as chairman of the faculty committee searching for a successor to President John Bennett at Union I was crushed between two forces at the seminary, a few on the faculty who were determined to have a certain candidate and the many who were equally determined not to have him. Again in that situation the students were manipulated and Christ crucified anew. My part in crucifying him was clear to me, a weakness of character in the face of intimidation, for which I still need forgiveness.

Jeremiah 38:1–6
Hebrews 13:1–16

In 586 B.C. and again in A.D. 70 the holy city of Jerusalem lay under siege. In the first instance the Babylonians successfully defeated the ancient Judahites and destroyed the inviolable city, and in the second instance the Romans successfully defeated the ancient Jews and destroyed the inviolable city. What is truly amazing about those two battles for Jerusalem is the prophetic literature which filtered through them and has come down to us out of them. The voices out of the past which Israel, both the old and the new, preserved were for the most part the voices which in their time had seemed intemperate, unpatriotic, scandalous, treasonous, and blasphemous.

Two such voices were those of Jeremiah during the time of the first siege, and of the anonymous author of the Epistle to the Hebrews in the time of the second siege. And I want to pair a saying of Jeremiah with one from Hebrews because I think they were saying approximately the same thing in analogous historical circumstances.

In Jeremiah's second trial, as recorded in chapter 38, during the worst of the final phases of the siege of Jerusalem, the prophet is charged with sedition and treason against the state and for undermining the patriotism of the soldiers and the citizens who had stayed to defend the city. In the trial Jeremiah is charged by the authorities for having said the following:

> He who stays in this city shall die by the sword, by famine, and by pestilence; but he who goes out to the Babylonians shall live. . . . This city shall surely be given into the hand of the army of the king of Babylon and be taken. [38:2–3]

The author of Hebrews, who was probably a refugee from the noble Roman efforts at the pacification of Jerusalem and Palestine (6:18), in his final exhortation to his constituency, who had perhaps fled with him, gives them advice very similar to that of Jeremiah over six centuries earlier:

> Therefore, let us go forth to him outside the camp, bearing abuse for him. For here we have no lasting city, but we seek the city which is to come. [13:13–14]

Both Jeremiah and Hebrews advised Israel to go "outside the camp," and they did so in times of upheaval and threat to the national existence. Jeremiah did so at a time when his fellow citizens and even his friends had no choice but to denounce him and testify against him. The people who at Jeremiah's first trial, as recorded in chapter 26, had defended him, in the second were aligned against him. The first trial had taken place at a time when the threat of siege and defeat was still rather remote, and Jeremiah's challenging judgments seemed no more than blasphemy against the concept of the inviolable holy city, serious enough in itself. But the second was precipitated when Jeremiah continued his persistent denunciations of the Jerusalem civil and cultic establishment in the face of imminent disaster. And all the liberals who had earlier defended his prophetic right of free speech now felt compelled to denounce him. Some of the names of those who testified against him the second time around (Shephatiah, Gedal-

iah, Jucal, Pashhur) were of families who had earlier been instru-
mental in helping him escape sentencing and the indignant mobs
after the first trial; and the princes who had earlier defended him
against the priests and prophets of the established cult, in the second trial were the ones who brought suit against him before the
king, saying: "Let this man be put to death, for he is weakening
the hands of the soldiers who are left in this city and the hands
of all the people, by speaking such words to them. For this man
is not seeking the welfare of this people, but their harm" (38:4).
And one can and must understand the position of such liberals.
Custodial liberals are by and large those whose role it is to defend
and protect the goods and gains of earlier struggles. It plainly
stood to reason, and their logic was unassailable, that neither
Jeremiah nor anyone else would have freedom of speech if the
Babylonians took over. There was no alternative for them at that
late date; they had to protect the structure as it was. For the
princes the property rights had to be protected at all costs because without retention of their God-given heritage, the promised
land of Canaan and the holy city of Jerusalem, there would then
be no way and no means to protect the human rights. It must
clearly be understood that they were not bad guys. On the contrary (like Pharaoh, Solomon, Zedekiah, Herod, and Pilate) they
were doing the very best they knew how by the best lights available to them. It was clearly impossible for the princes at that late
date to hear what Jeremiah was saying to them.

Jeremiah and Hebrews saw things differently from most of their
contemporaries and both advised all who would listen to go "outside the camp." Establishment religion, because of some of its best
theological traditions, always feels called upon to defend and protect what it considers its God-given heritage. Jeremiah and Hebrews, by contrast, and indeed the whole biblical prophetic tradition which they represent, insist that there must be no such
confusion between the Giver and the gift, but that there is nothing, nothing, nothing which falls outside God's transforming judgments. For them there was nothing among all God's gifts in all
of creation which was holy—holy in the sense that it could willy-
nilly escape God's judgments and the shaking of the foundations.
At the end of the previous chapter in Hebrews the author stressed

this point. In referring to the Exodus of ancient Israel and the *mysterium tremendum* of the Mt. Sinai experience he says, "God's voice then shook the earth; but now he has promised, 'Yet once more I will shake not only the earth but also the heaven.' This phrase, 'Yet once more,' indicates the removal of what is shaken, as of what has been made, in order that what cannot be shaken may remain" (12:26–27). "Our judge is the God of all" (12:23) and "Our God is a consuming fire" (12:29).

Jeremiah and Hebrews both distinguished between what Hebrews called shadow and reality. Hebrews, incidentally, has not in any sense borrowed a Platonic concept through Philo or anybody else; the author simply used a going idiom of his time to express in Greek a very fundamental point of biblical theology which Jeremiah had stated in his Iron Age Hebrew idiom with equal force: Truth lies in the order of the Creator, not in the order of the created. Nothing in all creation is holy; only God is holy.

For Jeremiah and Hebrews both, the true or the real Israel is in no way dependent on God's gifts to her. Jeremiah insisted that Israel had become so deceived into thinking that God was obligated to protect the national and cultic institutions which he had in an earlier era sponsored that Israel had become idolatrous with respect to those gifts and institutions. Despite Jeremiah's humane disposition, he knew that as long as the old Solomonic Temple stood, the people would be deceived into confusing symbols with reality. They had begun to accept the shadow for the real; they confused the gift and the Giver. "Look, teacher," some disciples once said to their master, "what wonderful stones and what beautiful buildings" (Mark 13:1). And so Jeremiah with naught but pain in his heart had come to the inescapable conclusion that attempts at reformation at that late date but increased the deception. Those who survive the sword, he said, must go out into the desert (outside the city, outside the camp) where God will appear to them from afar, embrace them, and say, "I have loved you with an everlasting love" (31:1–2). Jeremiah several times mentions this "God from afar," this "From-afar Yahweh," in contrast to the people's notion of the "Nearby Yahweh." It is clear that Jeremiah and Hebrews are saying very much the same thing:

in Christian idiom they were saying perhaps that God's coming (this intrusion of the Creator into the created, this strange mingling of the Ultimate amongst our petty penultimas) was not an incarceration in a temple nor in a holy city nor in a holy land nor indeed in a particular piece of real estate nor in a particular church, but an incarnation in a man. God is not hung up on what he has given us; he is hung up on us. Property rights is not his bag; people are his thing.

Against what were undoubtedly the jeers and taunts of non-Christians and anti-Christian polemicists in the first century who pointed out that these Christians had no proper religion, no temples or altars of priestly hierarchy, and were probably atheists anyway, the author of Hebrews in stately cadence claims (in 13:10), "We have an altar . . ." He meant of course the cross, for he goes on, in pursuit of the typology to the Day of Atonement sacrifice (Lev. 16:27) which was burnt outside the camp, to claim that Jesus suffered outside the camp (13:11–13), a patent reference to the crucifixion outside the city gates. He has many times claimed for Christians that their true sanctuary was located in heaven and their high priest was Christ; now he claims the cross as their altar. No, God is not hung up on what he has given us; he is hung up on us.

"Therefore, let us go forth to him outside the camp . . ." These prophetic voices bid us not to seek our identity in those present structures which God is challenging but in the embrace of the Giver. Jeremiah says God embraces us in everlasting love when we go outside the camp and surrender to the forces which threaten and challenge our idolatry; and Hebrews says that our true cult, our true religion, our altar is outside the camp, i.e., outside the establishment which crucified Christ because he had challenged it by his life and words and deeds.

But what about those inside the camp who remember the struggles of an earlier day and who know that iconoclasm in itself is as false as the idolatry it condemns? What about Jeremiah's friends in the sixth century and what of the good Pharisees and Essenes in the first? And again Jeremiah and Hebrews agree. What happened outside the camp is not the beginning of a new system, a new structure which simply moves further north or further left or further right, which must in its turn also be challenged. God, this "From-afar Yahweh," is always outside the camp. The Giver is never the gift and the gift is never the Giver. God's hang-up is not another cultic or political hangout. He's out there hung up on us precisely for the sake of all of us who have gotten hung up on his gifts.

"We have an altar [13:10]. . . . Therefore let us go forth to him outside the camp [13:13] . . ." into a mythical moment that never existed but exists even yet.

It is still dark. A weighty silence has fallen over the rock. The cries of pain and anguish are spent. The eyes of the onlookers are hollow and empty, dissipated in the horror they have come to witness. In stupor they turn away, each to his accustomed path, each to the soothing comforts of habit and home.

The spectacle has turned to obscenity. The attraction has become uncouth. The traitor, the seditious rebel, the dangerous politico, the messianic nuisance is now but a mangle of pain, a sorrow too personal any longer to gape upon. All eyes are averted now from the beauty of holiness which reaches out through the man on the cross. No one can any longer look.

The soldiers have finished their game. They have cast their lots. They too look away. This is the part they care for least, when the crucified one is dead and yet alive, wracked with the pain which only slowly yields to the merciful arms of approaching death. No matter how often he is assigned one of these crucifixions, the centurion cannot lightly look upon such anguish. "I don't ask for these jobs. I'm tough, sure, but I hate this detail. It wasn't my idea to crucify him; it never is my idea. I am a man under orders. When they tell me to crucify, I crucify. I obey orders. I always obey the orders they post for me. They'll never get me on insubordination."

Silence still. The man who drove the nails in pleads obedience as his defense. The soldier rightly obeyed his orders.

The soldiers withdraw a distance. At least they don't have to take the bodies down. Peter watches them closely until he feels that they won't see him in the darkness and confusion. He has to go to him this time. Turning to the cross he remembers all too well the look from the balcony at the high priest's house, and unable to look up he throws himself on the rock, inconspicuous.

"I had to tell them that I didn't know you. What earthly good would it have done to get myself arrested and implicate all the others as well? I was confused. We were all confused back in the garden. If we all ran away it was because, well, what could we do? The soldiers were armed. But I followed you to the court of the high priest, didn't I? Did I have to get arrested too, and get us all in trouble?"

Silence still. The disciple who denied him pleads the welfare of the group as his defense. Peter rightly thought of others as well as himself.

Peter pulls himself up and, broken, goes over and joins the women who wait. Pilate feels the darkness weigh upon him. The silhouette of the broken figure pierces the numbness, the overwhelming sense of incompetence which has flooded his soul. "Why couldn't I just go ahead and say 'Guilty' or 'Not guilty'? I don't know if he was or not, but why should I care? I feel so inadequate before these people. Why should I care if one is guilty or innocent? My hands are clean. I am not going to encourage any insurrection in my bailiwick. We must have law and order. My hands are clean. I'm innocent. I'm not involved. It's not just myself. I have to think of my position and of Rome. My hands are clean."

Silence still. The man who might have stopped it all but didn't, the man who kept Rome's good name out of it, pleads the higher importance of his office as his defense. Pilate rightly thought of his position as greater than himself.

Still torn and unsure, Judas tries to see his face, to read there some sign of right or wrong. "Was he or wasn't he? He wasn't my Messiah and that's for sure. But what was he? Caiaphas said he could only bring trouble on the nation and the church. But then he wasn't really a troublemaker. In fact he didn't stir up enough action for my money. God knows I loved him. Anyone who thinks it was easy to turn him over last night has never loved him or known him as I have. But some day a leader will arise and rid us of these damned Romans. I had hoped he would, but he wasn't the one. I couldn't take any more inaction, and Caiaphas assured me I was doing the right thing. But if you can't believe your priest, whom can you believe these days? The thirty pieces of silver will go far toward advancing our real war of independence against these Romans, these imperialist European colonialists. We'll get rid of them yet—with the right leader. Go home, Rome."

Silence still. The impatient activist who betrayed him pleads freedom's fight and the nationalist cause of independence as his defense. Judas rightly followed the advice of his bishop, and for services rendered received an honorarium.

Judas withdrew and Caiaphas came. Looking after Judas, Caiaphas thought, "He wants too much, that lad. He wants his war of independence immediately. He's impatient. The mills of God grind slowly. If he bore my responsibilities he wouldn't expect so much of people. God only knows what would have happened if I hadn't stopped this Galilean when I did. I don't have just a parish to oversee, I have a whole people, a whole church, and sometimes I simply have to step on some people's toes for the good of the whole. Why, if this latest Messiah had kept it up, Rome would have had no choice but to amass her armies and crush us. I couldn't let that happen. These *meshugoyyim* are more trouble than they're worth, going around as self-styled teachers and preachers talking about what God's going to do next. They're coming along about one a year now and, well, it's my job to stop them. If I didn't, we'd have chaos and the Roman armies on our necks. Without law and order there can be no viable society. I may not know exactly what God's going to do next but I have an idea what Rome would do if God does what these fellows say he'll do. And I'm not about to pit God against Caesar. It's a thankless job being bishop of a people like this. God knows I do what I can to keep his people from getting crushed into oblivion. I guess that's what I'm high priest for and I guess that's what I'll keep on doing—trying to keep the church going."

Silence still. And as the darkness lifts, Caiaphas leaves Golgotha to join Annas at the manse by Zion. The priest who had to choose between a single man and the whole people pleads the responsibility of his office as his defense. Caiaphas rightly saved both church and state from disaster.

After Caiaphas has come a line two centuries long in this mythical moment that did not exist and yet exists eternally, a line of humanity to the cross, to this altar outside the camp, each man with his own defense and excuse, each with his brief prepared. After Caiaphas might have come John, perhaps, and the other disciples to explain why they ran away, why they forsook him to the soldiers in the garden. (They couldn't have done anything.) Each man must come, and each man has his defense, and each defense is unassailable.

But he just keeps on hanging there. Why doesn't he pass judgment on us, sentence us, punish us and get it over with instead of accepting us as we are, discounting our pleas, brushing aside our defenses, knocking every prop from under us? Our excuses, our pleas are sound and good, but he won't accept them; he accepts us instead. Why must he love us so and strip us bare? Why must he forgive us so and leave us so naked?

"We have an altar. . . . Therefore, let us go forth to him outside the camp . . ."

8. It Is Finished

"It Is Finished" was written in the late winter of 1958 for delivery in the chapel at Colgate Rochester Divinity School where I was at the time assistant professor of Old Testament. I had been assigned chapel duty for a Thursday service late in Lent. Thursday's was the high service of the week in those days, followed by an "all-school luncheon." It was traditionally the big day of the week for the seminary community. One always took it seriously, at least to the point of writing sermons especially for the occasion. At that time I had not much of a "barrel" anyway to draw upon.

In late February playing handball in the gym I had suffered a rather severe lumbo-sacral muscular strain. For the pain, which was considerable, my doctor had prescribed medicine with some form of codeine in it. This sermon was composed in first draft during a winter's evening while sitting in my study in my beloved barcalounger floating one inch above the pain. It came all at once, as it were in a rush. The lead idea once conceived was simple: whatever is said by anyone is perhaps heard and understood in as many different ways as there are people to hear it, especially if it touches their lives existentially.

One must remember that Protestant theology in the fifties in America was heavily neoorthodox (whatever that means), with considerable effort to appropriate existentialist thinking. Politically, campus and church life were relatively quiet. Most of us worked for Stevenson at election times, notably the following fall, but we were not greatly upset with Eisenhower, simply impressed with his naiveté. Preacher Roe was pitching for the Dodgers in season; Y. A. Tittle was leading the football Giants to a series of autumn victories despite the humiliation delivered them by that fellow over in Baltimore, Johnny Something-or-other, in sudden-death overtime in the fabulous new Super Bowl; and Frank Gifford was bringing style to professional football to the pride of young America. These were as much concerns in those days as the Sinai Campaign, or Prague, or distant Korea of the early fifties. The population explosion was coming to the fore as well as ecology, but the latter was an unknown word to most of us still. Nay, they were halcyon days in many ways. Our colleague William Hamilton had not yet conceived of divine mortality but was still fighting the old-time liberals on the Rochester faculty with every new volume of Barth's *Dogmatics* translated into English.

To preach a sermon in a liberal setting suggesting that nobody near the cross understood what Jesus was trying to say could create a stir of sorts. To suggest therein that only the angels in heaven saw the whole and could put the evil, injustice, and suffering of Good Friday into a larger perspective was received by most as beautiful in a poetic sort of way but unreal. Still the response was amazing. Bill Hamilton came by after chapel to say that he thought it perhaps the most moving expression of a position he could not hold he had heard. (That was the sort of relation Bill and I had.)

My wife gave a copy soon after it was first published later that spring (*Colgate Rochester Divinity School Bulletin* 30 (1958): 70–74) to Thomas S. Canning, a composer at the Eastman School of Music in Rochester, whose experience with it turned out to be much like my own. It apparently caught his imagination, for he soon thereafter brought her a score of music corresponding to the text, which he had composed during the course of a night, finishing it just before dawn. The music was conceived by Canning as in dialogue with the descriptions in the sermon of the existential reactions of the ten humans, or groups of people, who might have heard Jesus' cry from the cross, and of course with that of the angels at the end. In form he created a dialogue between speaker and organist. The score also calls at one point for a drum.

My wife in turn created dances in a Doris Humphrey–Jose Limon style to suit the musical intervals. We went thereafter to many college campuses and not a few churches performing the whole. Dora, my wife, was at the time on the faculty of the University of Rochester teaching interpretive dance. The musical score has unfortunately never been published, and of course the dances, not labanotated, exist yet only in Dora's memory. The sermon as such was published a second time in *The Pulpit* 30 (1959): 81–83, and it showed up in modified form as a chapter in a little book I published in 1961 (*The Old Testament in the Cross* [New York: Harper & Row, Publishers], pp. 110–22).

Part of the inspiration for the close of the sermon came from appreciation of Max Beckmann's (1884–1950) painting *The Descent from the Cross* (1917), in the Museum of Modern Art in New York. The bulk of the canvas centers in the removal of Christ's mutilated body from the cross. The blood, pain, and gore are all there, but so is a ladder which rests on one of the crossbars used in the "descent." Eventually one's eye rises to observe with growing light that the ladder does not stop but goes on up and up into heaven: the descent of the body from the cross is but a part of the condescension of the incarnation. It soon occurs to the observer that the full significance of that sad and tragic moment of defeat and grief cannot be appreciated except as it is put into its proper setting, the whole story of God's amazing grace from beginning to end. Those privy to observe from the top of the ladder down, the angels "with fiery eyes downcast," would have known: they would have known the full meaning of "It is finished."

When Jesus had received the vinegar, he said, "It is finished"; and he bowed his head and gave up his spirit.

John 19:30

What does it mean, this word *tetelestai*? According to John it accompanies the very expiration of Jesus' last breath. What does it mean? There are so many possibilities.

To be critically honest we should not find too much in the Greek verb *teleo*, meaning "accomplish" or "come to an end." Franz Delitzsch in his translation of the New Testament into Hebrew (1880) uses undoubtedly the mot juste when he translates it *kullah*—"It is finished." The form critics are probably right in seeing these so-called "last seven words" as later accretions. If we are interested in what really happened we must probably be satisfied with the likelihood of a simple outcry of pain and anguish. What the evangelists are trying to say, as so often elsewhere in the Gospels, is that the Crucifixion fits into the divine pattern. The point that had first to be established for the faith and mission of the church was that this Crucifixion was not just another that Josephus might chronicle alongside that of the eight hundred Pharisees whom Alexander Jannaeus crucified in 88 B.C. or those crucified in the War of Varus in 4 B.C. This was no accident of history.

In other words the Crucifixion is not at all what it seems to be a tragedy of life, another case of a good man unjustly accused, a miscarriage of human justice. Far from that, it is the true statement of divine judgment on all mankind. Yet more and at the same time it is the true statement of divine grace. God did not conquer sin and solve man's predicament by fighting evil with evil but by conquering evil with suffering love. Simply put, they wanted simply to say, This is not only a fact of history, this is the true sovereignty of God.

Then what is meant by *tetelestai*—"It is finished"? From the days of slavery we inherit the spiritual "Were you there when they crucified my Lord?" One of the outstanding factors in the cultic rites of Old Testament Israel was the act of remembrance, which we call today *anamnēsis*. By this cultic principle Israel saw herself reflected in the stories which made up her cultic, or holy, history. For instance by this principle later Israel claimed for herself in each generation the experience of the Exodus or the vicissitudes and victories of Abraham and Jacob. Thus there was the sense of corporate personality whereby the patriarch Jacob was Israel latent or the people Israel were Jacob patent. The pattern of the interpersonal tensions between Jacob and Esau was the pattern of intertribal and international relations between Israel and Edom, or other nations. The blessings of Jacob (Genesis 49) or Moses (Deuteronomy 33) upon the twelve patriarchs became little mirrors wherein the later tribes saw themselves well reflected. By the same principle the church finds itself reflected in the gospel story. It is remarkable how the vicissitudes and victories of the twelve disciples are a portrait of the church since that time. Let us look carefully into the mirror which the last moment of Jesus' life affords to see if perhaps the world has ever really escaped that moment or if in some sense we must not hear for ourselves the anguished cry "It is finished."

Suppose we gather about the cross and observe the reactions of those the Passion account tells us heard or might have heard this fearsome cry. We are told in Matthew that at Jesus' final word the curtain of the Temple was torn in two and in the Gospel to the Hebrews that a large lintel of the Temple fell down. Nature's response to this divine judgment was as in the prophets in concert with the curse, a fall of darkness at midday. Nature's response is therefore in the early Christian cultus clear and sharp. What was man's response? What meaning did it have, this awesome cry, to those present, those who were "there when they crucified my Lord"?

There were the two thieves, the one desperate for his life, whose last hope of clinging to an empty existence was this teacher, this man of whom he had heard as the Christ. "Save yourself and us!" Let's see you make good your claims. Like the tempter in the desert at the start of Jesus' career this man at the end of his life challenges Jesus to show his supernatural powers. But all Jesus could respond was "It is finished." Disappointment and derision were the reaction of the first thief: Yeah, it's over but good. I knew you couldn't do anything for anybody anyway. You're a big joke, Jesus. All life's one big joke. And we hear his raucous, derisive but frightened laughter pierce our own doubting hearts.

There was the second thief and the centurion. Their reaction was much the same. "We are receiving the due reward of our deeds; but this man has done nothing wrong" is the rebuke of the so-called "good thief" to his weak companion. Likewise the centurion, according to Luke, said, "Certainly this man was innocent." These two statements represent at least the reaction of most men since that day. Jesus' Crucifixion is history's prime example of the miscarriage of justice, the innocent oppressed and unjustly accused. This is humanism at its best: the cross is man's sin, his inability because of his own fears and insecurity to insure justice's true balance and right execution, that trapped in his own fears and ambitions man yet fails to guarantee his own rights and dignity. "Certainly this man was innocent," says the centurion to our shame and to our failure.

Then there were the Roman soldiers. It was noon, they say, when they crucified him. Assigned to a detail they did their job. "And they crucified him." A soldier doesn't ask why he drew this or that assignment; he does what he is ordered to do. "And they crucified him." Nasty job to pull. But somebody has to. When your number's up your number's up. "And they crucified him." Wretched day. Hot. Humid. Cloudy. Storm brewing. Anybody for a quick game? "And they cast lots to divide his garments." Thirsty! Listen to that one. He's thirsty! Who in hades isn't on a damnable day like this? Here, give him some of that vinegar they throw out on their Passover—that'll show him a thirst! If you are the king of the Jews, get out of this one—if you can! Not exactly a kingly brew, a royal potion. "Father, forgive them." "It is finished." A bad job; but it's over now. "It is finished." Another day, another shekel.

Annas and Caiaphas heard it, and so did their legal advisors. A close call on that one. Seditious rebel. Can't afford to have the Romans on our necks for the likes of him. Jeopardize the whole nation? Not on his life! King of Israel indeed! But it's over now. Case of the traitor Jesus closed. It's finished.

The crowd dwindles. The shouting subsides. Wagging their heads they snort and chuckle. Destroy the temple! Who did he think he was? Rebuild it in three days! He fancied himself at playing Solomon. Good riddance, I say. That was a good one. But it's finished now.

Somewhere in the shadows lurked a freed man. Released from prison, his first day out of jail. Barabbas delivered from bondage! Term of sentence finished.

Off in the distance on the palace balcony stand Pilate and his wife. A nightmare come true, but after all—I didn't really know him. It wasn't as though he were somebody important. What's done's done. "What I have written I have written," says he. Call the houseboy and have him remove this bowl and make sure he cleans the ring around the bowl. If there is anything I can't stand, says he, it's a dirty washbowl. The towel too. I like things neat and trim, nothing half done, you know. And that's that. It is finished.

Back in the shadows on the hill a few remain. The disciples and the women. The tragic end of a noble adventure. Everything seemed fine last night at supper. I gave up my fishing, my whole life to follow him. And it comes to this. What went wrong? What happened? Nothing means anything anymore. You bet your life on the best you know and then this. It's all over. All I've believed in, everything I've put my faith in. It is finished. Disillusionment. Disappointment. Tragedy. Return to Galilee and return to trying to make a living fishing. That's all there is now. It is finished.

Down the hill a way stands a husky fellow, a field laborer looking pensively at the figure on the cross. Simon of Cyrene says to himself, I thought it would help a bit to carry the cross. I didn't realize until now the hardest part: to have the cross carry you. Just to hang there. Poor fellow. I guess he's glad it *is* finished. *He* had the rough part. Just hanging there. It's good it is all over now; a body just couldn't take much more. It's finished.

All kinds of people look for the kingdom of God, like Joseph, the one from Arimathea. A pious man if ever there was one. A member of a local small town sanhedrin. You can't blame him though. He didn't have anything to do with this. He's against capital punishment in the first place, and not only that, he couldn't be sure about Jesus—he was looking for the kingdom of God. But too late now. Nothing now to say or do for that matter but bury the remains. Well, that we can do in proper style. The best tomb available, the finest shrouds—pile the flowers high. Better late than never. The finish it is.

But in the stillness of eternity did you ever hear a heart break? In the chill of infinity did you ever hear the heart of God break? I have given the beloved of my soul into the hand of the enemy.

But it is finished. God broke his own heart and it was finished. The love of God pursued us everyone to that hill where the cross stands. What does it mean to us that it is finished? Not with armies celestial or apocalyptic cataclysm, not with swords loud clashing nor vengeance, not rebuke nor justice nor just deserts: the strife is o'er, the battle done! It is finished. Love pursued sin and evil, corruption, ignorance, rebellion, and pride all the way to Calvary and nailed them to the cross. We have done our worst. Man can do no worse than he has already done. It is finished. No Enochian Son of man appearing in the clouds with angelic armies won this battle. No, God just broke his heart. And it is finished.

> The strife is o'er, the battle done;
> The victory of life is won;
> The song of triumph has begun,
> *It is finished!*
> The powers of death have done their worst,
> But Christ their legions has dispersed;
> Let shouts of holy joy outburst,
> *It is finished!*

"Then I looked, and I heard around the throne . . . the voice of many angels, and the number of them was ten thousand times ten thousand and thousands of thousands, saying with a loud voice, 'Worthy is the Lamb who was slain to receive power and riches and wisdom and might and honor and glory and blessing.' And I heard every creature in heaven and on earth and under the earth and in the sea saying, 'To him who sits upon the throne and to the Lamb be blessing and honor and glory and might forever and ever!' " Amen.

9. Through Shattered Concrete Slabs

Easter 1967. There was turmoil all about, increasing in intensity. Many people were beginning to say that the fabric of society and culture as we had known them in America was splitting at the seams. Things were coming apart, it seemed. Those who had worked in the system and benefited from it, like my friends at the Brick Church in Rochester, were threatened but were still able for the most part to bracket what disturbed them as passing hysteria. Good Christians knew there was evil in the world, but there were several ways of dealing with it, and these did not include spotlighting it and giving it center stage. Those who did so were felt to be immature and naive.

It is interesting that that seems to be the prevalent attitude now, more than a decade later. Eldridge Cleaver is now a charismatic Christian working in the system. Even Mark Rudd has come out of fugitive hiding to face charges against him. The Weather Underground has surfaced and is clearly split asunder. Who was right? Who was wrong? Moral indignation ran high, however, even among those who did not want to destroy the beast, as many students put it. And that moral indignation lies close beneath the surface even today among many who are otherwise quiescent. Students in many parts of the world are expressing it in the manner of the sixties even if in America most campuses are quiet.

There can be little doubt that many students were self-serving in their rebellion. The economy was good in large measure because of the war, and employment was high. They could rebel and still get jobs, they thought. The system could take some pounding and still produce its wonderful benefits, maybe even reform a bit. And there was the draft to evade. Much moral indignation on the part of many male students was fed by the desire to stay out of the Vietnam War in personal ways. Some students enrolled in seminaries, it would appear, to secure a ministerial deferment and maybe exemption.

But some of us felt that there could have been no justice whatever on earth if somebody had not cried out a loud no to some of the insanity in the world, even if the ones crying were not totally mature or pure. This does not mean that we thought they were right and the older generation wrong. It is simply undeniable that some highly placed responsible officials were trapped in their contexts and needed to hear a challenging voice. Sure, the students were trapped in their contexts too, and their arrogance often outdistanced that of anyone over thirty. And we faculty were trapped between them and the trustees, the system par excellence. We sometimes tried to mediate only to find ourselves accused by both sides of being part of the problem and contributing to it. The students called us hirelings of the insensitive rich and the board members accused us of misleading the students to their rebellious ways. One does wonder where those students are who helped destroy some of the right and good things in university and campus life: they have perhaps melded into the systemic mass, no more repentant than the insensitive rich.

Rochester had had its riots back in the summer of 1964. Pride was wounded but rapidly recovering. Rochester was still the best city God had founded on earth—a few faults, yes, but still Rochester. Saul Alinsky and FIGHT were a disturbing thorn in many sides still (see the introduction to chapter 5 above), but the focus in the spring of 1967 was considerably more on Vietnam and the protests at home against it than on racial injustice in cities. The two evils were mixed in many minds, inseparable monsters joined at the spleen of Americanism. In other minds, Communism had to be contained even at great expense of wealth and lives since it was a far greater evil than anything at home. And unfortunately, many Christians nurtured on a totally false and inverted ethic of election (and not a few Presbyterians) believed in some form of meritocracy: God does not fool around; those who are blessed of this world's goods obviously have divine favor, while the poor and indigent must somehow deserve their low estate. After all, if one was poor in wonderful America it had to be one's own fault! How could it be otherwise?

Students, young people generally, and some others tried to say it was otherwise. The best of their voices expressed a chiding and challenging hope that change was blowing in the wind. "Now it's starting . . ." wrote Tom Sankey. And poets like Amos Wilder, a perceptive theologian, could write, "An elder charity breaks through these modern fates . . ."

Easter was a time for Christians to remember, whether they were more disturbed by injustice or by the seemingly chaotic voices raised against it, that God is not stumped by human folly but can mold it into cosmic purpose, ultimate truth, and good. Wilder had a couple of years earlier published a poem expressive of Easter hope, a hope powerful enough not only to roll away stones but to shatter even our modern prison walls and concrete slabs of cold inhumanity. He called it "The Third Day."

Dr. David A. MacLennan, who had been pastor at Brick since 1955, had just left for Pompano Beach, Florida, and our good friends at Brick invited us back from New York where we had moved in 1965, to celebrate Easter with them. The Easter service at Brick in those days was a festival in about as High Church a mode as Presbyterians permit themselves. Many parts of the service would have been typical of earlier Easters as well. But there was one major surprise: in the midst of the sermon on prearranged cue the choir sang Bob Dylan's "Blowing in the Wind," accompanied by a couple of youthful guitarists. The service included Wilder's poem in full (italics mine).

THE THIRD DAY

The immovable stone tossed aside,
The collapsed linens,
The blinding angel and the chalky guards:
All today like an old woodcut.

The earthquake on the third day,
The awakened sleeper,
The ubiquitous stranger, gardener, fisherman:
Faded frescoes from a buried world.

Retell, renew the event
In these planetary years,
For we were there and He is here:
It is always the third day.

Our world-prison is split;
An elder charity
Breaks through these modern fates.
Publish it by Telstar,
Diffuse it by mundovision.

He *passes through the shattered concrete slabs,*
The vaporized vanadium vaults,
The twisted barbed-wire trestles.

A charity coeval with the suns
Dispels the deep obsessions of the age,
And opens heart-room in our sterile dream:
A new space within space to celebrate

With mobiles and new choreographies,
A new time within time to set to music.°
                          Amos Niven Wilder

Resurrection in the Bible is not a private affair or an individual experience but an act of God. It is first and foremost a sign of God's sovereign presence. The Resurrection of Jesus speaks not so much of the divinity of Jesus but, like the Incarnation, emphasizes the humanity of God—that is, the decisive presence of God with men. The ancient Pharasaic Jewish doctrine of the resurrection of the dead was always and still is the sign of the awful presence of God. Unfortunately the history of the Christian handling of the question of resurrection has centered in (a) whether Jesus' Resurrection really happened and (b) if so, citing it as the proof of the claims of Christianity. But the Resurrection testifies to the immediate, burning, judging, and redeeming presence of God; its purpose is not to justify our risk of faith. The Resurrection on the contrary but confirms what we already knew by the Incarnation: it is God who confronted us and confronts us in Christ Jesus.

In and through everything in the New Testament we must constantly ask the question, What is God doing, what does this or that say of God, what is the nature of God as he reveals himself in Christ? In the neoorthodox generation immediately past, there was a valiant but rather parochial effort to find Christ in the Old Testament. In the coming period of theocentric pluralism I think we will witness a search for God in the New.

In the Bible Resurrection is the counterpart of Creation. The biblical argument is very simple: if God can create he can certainly re-create; if God can give life in the first place he can give it again. The Bible refuses any form of cosmic dualism. God is the God of light and darkness, good and evil, weal and woe, life and death. He is transcendent to our experience of birth and death. He is not trapped in the natural cycle or in the historical cycle,

*Copyright 1965 Christian Century Foundation. Reprinted by permission from the April 14, 1965 issue of *The Christian Century*; reprinted in *Grace Confounding: Poems by Amos Niven Wilder* (Philadelphia: Fortress Press, 1972), p. 3.

the world prison in which we are bound. His presence with man does not mean his subjection to nature or history but rather his judgment of both, his cutting across both. God's transcendence is not up there, down there, back there, or out there anywhere; God's transcendence is his presence among men in history, which cuts across all of the laws to which man is subject and in which he is bound. The Resurrection of Christ is God's ultimate transcendent presence within this world prison of nature and history. God's presence, in this ever present resurrection, is a transcendent crack across the totality of human experience. It is his judgment of the best we know and do and say and think in any generation. It is a judging and promising crack in the prison walls of our presuming that we have all the answers. It is precisely a stone rolled from the tomb of man's deceptive entrapment. The Resurrection tells the truth which challenges the truths which we extrapolate from nature and history. It is the judgment of tomorrow's discovery on today's ignorance. It is the saving judgment of God's contradicting presence in the midst of our petit established truths. He who was "party to the savage passion of creation that spawned the countless stars and thrust the cold rock mountains up from boiling seas" *can* pass through all our shattered concrete slabs. It was his nature from before time began to roll stones where he willed and shatter the slabs of every human folly. To believe in the Resurrection of Christ is not to claim that we Christians are somehow right so to believe but rather to assert that by that Resurrection we are judged and thus saved, by him "who sprung the soaring arch of life and built the colonnade of time."

The Resurrection is the hope of those who have learned the awful truth of human weakness and folly. Why is it that the innocent, the immature, and the poor seem to believe in miracles when we responsible folk of course know better? Could it be that they believe out of the necessity of hope? Could it be that they believe not because they are ignorant but because being at the bottom of the social scale they have a sharper, more poignant view of human fear and folly? Could it be that because they have so little hope in life as they see it close about them, they are drawn to the hope they perceive in the crack in the laws of nature to which the miracle attests? If natural law can thus be violated, there is hope that the laws of human existence can also be broken and violated. If the system of nature can develop a crack and let God's light shine through, then perhaps the systems of human order and existence can also develop a crack and let the light of hope shine through. All God's shattering cracks by which he breaks into our human existence are the challenge of his judgments which alone can save us.

The common thinking of Western man since the Renaissance and the subsequent flow of the world's wealth into the Western world has been to deprecate theism and exalt humanism. But the prophets and Jesus never tired in pointing out that such wealth, comfort, and power blind man's vision and prevent his seeing the folly of thinking that man is the final judge of what is true. Could it be that those outside the power structures and patterns of human intercourse, precisely those who believe that the systems can be cracked, are those capable of perceiving truth?

Could it be on the other hand that the young people of the world, the fifty percent of the world under the age of responsibility, can see a transcending crack which we cannot see? Senator Kennedy pointed out in his speech in Philadelphia on February 24th that "more and more of our children are almost unreachable by the familiar premises and arguments of our adult world."[*] They seem to want to wear their clothes and their hair only in those styles which we cannot approve. It is all well and good for us historians to say their trousers have to get a lot tighter before they are as tight as our grandfathers' or George Washington's, or their hair has to get a lot longer before it gets as long as the young Ben Franklin's; these styles go in cycles, of course. But we also have to notice that the style change these days is expressive of something more than growing up. The young people seem to us to devise dance steps they know we cannot take over or approve of; dance steps which in our day we would blushingly have called bumps and grinds are now essential parts of the Frug and Watusi. The filthy speech movement has become so widespread that we can no longer compare it to our own growing-up escapades or wild-oats sowing or giggles behind the barn. They seem to want to shock us and alienate us. But what are they saying to

---

[*]Robert F. Kennedy, "What Can the Young Believe?" *New Republic*, 11 March 1967, pp. 11–12. I am indebted to the senator for a number of the ideas and phrases in the following paragraphs.

us? No one, least of all they, can deny that the men at the top
of our social and political institutions have all the information
about this or that particular situation which the rest of us lack.
But our children seem to reject the premises and arguments and
presuppositions through which all that information is being
filtered.

Some of the bearded youth refer to themselves as Christ-haired
or Jesus-bearded. And we are immediately shocked and offended.
They seem to want to offend us and outrage us mainly because
they despair of ever understanding us: Our piety in refusing to
reform abortion laws they find inconsistent with our support of
killing (innocent) Vietnamese by the thousands. We may try to
explain the situation to them but they see us say, "Abortion no,
bombing yes," and they feel that we are the zombies of another
Stone Age.

The following "Poet's Monologue" from Scene 10 of Tom
Sankey's "Golden Screw" is a typical expression among many
young people today.

> Listen to the sound of change. I don't mean the electric tinny
> boom music sound, although that's part of it. . . . I mean the
> pulsing, throbbing rumbling sound of change.
>
> There is a revolution going on. And I don't mean the civil rights
> thing or the peace thing or the turning on routine or serving
> drinks to deviants bit, but something bigger, something under-
> neath, something pushing all these other things ahead of it.
>
> It's more than revolution, it's evolution! It's happening *now*. The
> freaks of the world are seen to be normal and the madness that
> has held the world is dissolving. The cosmic consciousness is
> groping its way into every brainpan and some will embrace it with
> whoops of joy and some will lock it out with grunts of dry disgust,
> but the movement continues through everwidening avenues of the
> great life! Now it's starting and before its tremendous cellular
> boom the ages of cold hard rusty rotten barriers will be tumbled
> and shredded and fed to the fires of the first life . . .°

I speak now not of the beatniks and those whom we stolid
citizens reject even before we hear what they say; I speak rather
of the hundred student body presidents and editors of college

---

°Tom Sankey, "Golden Screw," an unpublished play performed at the
Provincetown Theatre on MacDougal Street in Greenwich Village. I am
indebted to Mr. Sankey for providing me a typescript of the monologue.

newspapers, the thousands of former Peace Corps volunteers, the dozens of Rhodes scholars who question the basic premises of the Vietnam War. They seem not to be able to accept Josef Stalin's propaganda, which we accepted, that Communism is a monolithic structure.* They do not see the evidence for our fear of a worldwide Communist conspiracy. They live in the coming era of pan-pluralism. They see the world as one in which Communist states can be each others' deadliest enemies, or even friends of the West, a world in which Communism is certainly no better but perhaps no worse than many other evil and repressive dictatorships all around the world—with which we conclude alliances to contain Communism. Could it be that their view that Communism is the biggest fraud perpetrated in the history of human political institutions is right? Could it be they have seen a crack? No, their view is immature, we say.

They see us devastate the land of a people we call our friends. And however it may seem to us, they see it as one in which the largest and most powerful nation on earth is killing children (they do not care if accidentally) in a remote and insignificant land. We speak of conspiracies and commitments, of the burden of past mistakes, but they ask why they should now atone for mistakes made before many of them were born, before almost any of them could vote. Could it be that theirs are the mouths of babes speaking wisdom to our folly? Could it be they have seen a crack? No, they don't know of the realities of life; they will grow up, we say.

They see us who control half of the world's wealth spend billions on armaments while poverty and ignorance continue all over the world. They see us willing to fight a war for freedom in Southeast Asia but unwilling to fight with one-hundredth the money or force or effort to secure freedom in Mississippi or Alabama or the ghettos of the North. They see us get the so-called peace jitters and wonder if Wall Street doubts it can afford peace. But they ask if this shrinking world can afford a hungry, war-torn Asia; or if Western social and political institutions can afford to condone the despair of thirteen million blacks under apartheid in South Africa. The next generation will surely find out for us

*The central point of Max Frankel's article "Can We End the Cold War?" *New York Times Magazine*, 29 January 1967, pp. 20ff.

whether man can adapt to the demands of peace. Could it be that Isaiah was right that a young child shall lead them? Could it be they have seen a crack? No, the young are always idealistic, we say.

They think of labor as grown sleek and bureaucratic with power, sometimes frankly discriminatory, occasionally even corrupt and exploitative—a force not for change but for the status quo, unwilling or unable to organize new groups of members, indifferent to the men who once worked the coal mines of Appalachia, a latecomer to the struggles of the grape pickers of California or the farm laborers of the Mississippi Delta. Could it be that a twelve-year-old dumbfounded the doctors in the Temple? Could it be they have seen a crack? No, they simply do not know the hard route labor has had to come these fifty years, we say.

The commonest theme in the history of mankind is that of heroic rebels becoming in their turn and by their successes the next oppressors. Castro the hero of the Cuban mountain retreats once established in Havana became a different Castro, a victim of the arrogance of power. The United States, the leader of the world's modern revolutions, now finds itself (and we do not honestly quite know how—for there are no bad guys in history) in league with those dictatorships in the world which will call themselves anti-Communist. And the young people say that they cannot see any difference between the Fascist dictators and the Communist dictators—except that one seems to be determined by terror to protect investments and landholdings while the other seems to be determined by terror to carry through land reform. Could it be they have seen a crack? No, they will grow up and become mature, like us, we say.

Could it be that in our determination to punish what we view as aggression and to contain Communism, and in Ho's determination to fight for what he views as the preservation of the union of North and South Vietnam, that both our hearts like Pharaoh's have been hardened so that this horrible image which we do not like any more than they, of a huge, powerful nation trying to punish one of the poorest and smallest because of ideological chalk lines, may be burned forever into man's historic memory?

Could it be that there *is* a kingdom where only the meek and those like children can enter it? No, they will mature and see that this is the war to prevent future guerrilla wars, we say.

Could it be that the young are right and change *is* possible, and the cruelties and follies and injustices of the world will yield, however grudgingly, to the sweat and sacrifice they are so ready to give, as is evidenced by the heroism of our troops as well as the courage of our dissenters? Could it be that they have perceived the dire necessity of the transcending crack in the concrete slabs which we adults in Moscow, Peking, London, and Washington have erected between East and West, between Communist and capitalist, between Jew and Arab, between Semite and gentile, between white and black, between the old and the young, between the familiar and the strange? Could it be that they have perceived the falsehood in homogeneity and the possibilities of truth in heterogeneity, dialogue, and conversation? Could it be that *they* are prepared to love *our* enemies, as our risen Lord commanded? Could it be they have seen a crack in the concrete slabs of human fear and folly? Could it be that they have seen a stone rolled away?*

> Retell, renew the event
> In these planetary years,
> For we were there and He is here;
> It is always the third day.
>
> Our world-prison is split;
> An elder charity
> Breaks through these modern fates. . . .
>
> He passes through the shattered concrete slabs,
> The vaporized vanadium vaults,
> The twisted barbed-wire trestles.

"Now on the first day of the week Mary Magdalene came early to the tomb while it was still dark, and saw that the stone had been rolled away . . ."

It could be. It could be.

---

*At this point in the sermon the choir, with guitar accompaniment, sang "Blowing in the Wind" by Bob Dylan.

Conclusion: A Biblical Paradigm— The Torah-Christ Story

There is no claim in the foregoing that there is but one way to view the Bible or only one way to expound it in the believing communities today. On the contrary we have stressed the pluralism within the Bible itself. One of the reasons the Bible has lasted so long and given survival power to synagogue and church at numerous crucial junctures in their histories is surely its pluralism, its inherent depths of ambiguity (in the right sense of that term) and especially its adaptability as canon. There is nothing built upon what it says that can escape the challenge of something else in it: it contains its own built-in correctives. Every program of obedience which has issued from genuine dialogue with the Bible but then goes on to become a rigid, oppressing structure itself eventually comes under the judgment of the very canon out of which that structure had first blossomed.

The sermons presented here have stressed the corrective powers of the Bible, those which challenge the "obedient" and offer redemptive power for what has gone wrong with what was right. When Israel itself attains some power of its own and becomes someone else's Egypt, then there emerges from the Bible itself a way to read what it says as a challenge to those forms of static obedience which blind even the faithful. These pages have stressed the hermeneutic of prophetic critique which emerges from critical study of the Bible itself. It is not the only way to read the Bible, but it is one very important way to do so.

The context into which the Bible is to be read and interpreted indicates the basic hermeneutic axiom the interpreter should use in explicating any passage in it. Nearly all the contexts in which I have preached indicated the hermeneutic of prophetic critique: hence the above efforts emerged out of attempting to seek in various biblical passages the blessings needed by white American, rather affluent congregations. And those needs, far from being further encouragement to think what the people already thought or do what they were already doing (or not doing), were clearly the challenge which the Bible can amply supply to those whom power corrupts. One of the wonderful things about the corruption of thinking which even a modicum of power induces is the blindness that accompanies it. I have never known a people, a congregation, a nation, or any group to be able clearly to see its own corruption of thinking. Our Lord put it in terms of motes and logs in eyes. Isaiah had put it in terms of fatness about the heart. Never, never, never has the prophet who brought the challenge been elected to popular post by those he challenged. It is always left to the next generations to discern the power of prophetic speech. In the popular terms of today we must say that Martin Luther King, Jr., was not a prophet for his own people. Far from it, he was the greatest encouragement to them to do what they had been wanting to do that most of them had ever known. He was a Moses leading his people out of social and economic serfdom, but not a prophet in the Amos-Jeremiah-Jesus sense. His words and deeds had a prophetic challenging effect on white America (see chapter 2); but he did not use prophetic hermeneutic in applying the Bible to his own people's situation. Instead he used a constitutive hermeneutic, and he used it as effectively as any interpreter has ever done. He brought the Bible (or certain passages in it) to his people as a supportive power in their struggle for justice in the American context.

Discernment of context as well as of the biblical text read and interpreted in it cannot be overstressed in our situation today any more than it can be overstressed in attempting to recover the points the ancient biblical writers and thinkers scored in their contexts. The conjunction of ancient text and ancient context indicates the hermeneutics the ancient thinker used, just as the discernment of modern context and text indicates the hermeneutics the contemporary interpreter should use. The Bible is full of unrecorded hermeneutics which only the tools of biblical criticism can ferret out. It is the thesis here that those same hermeneutics may continue to be used today if dynamically conceived and applied. The sermons in this book have attempted to do so.

The hermeneutic techniques employed here were dynamic analogy, the concept of memory or re-presentation today of tension and resolution in the biblical accounts, looking for mirrors of identity rather than models for morality in the biblical stories, employing the three Hs—honesty, humility, and humor—in attempting to bring the stories alive rightly today, and finally, viewing the Bible as paradigm.

If the Bible as canon in the believing communities is seen not as a box of jewels of wisdom forever of static value but rather as a paradigm of how God thinks and acts in and through and across the several cultures out of which the Bible arose, then it will of necessity be read and appreciated quite differently than otherwise. This means that upon reading a biblical passage it is mandatory to theologize first and then thereupon, out of that effort, to derive suggestions for obedience. It means quite clearly that in reading a biblical passage we cannot first moralize.[1] The Bible is not a guarantor of the eternal value of old Bronze or Iron Age ethics, nor indeed of the mores of the hellenistic period from which the New Testament sprang. We can do a Paul on Paul, as it were. If Paul views the Torah story as good, holy, and eternal but the Torah stipulations as abrogated, then by dynamic analogy we can view Paul's gospel as good and holy but his ethics as abrogated.[2] We must work out our own ethics in our own contexts guided by a dynamic reading of the gospel of God's works from Genesis through the New Testament, with fear and trembling (Phil. 2:13).

Viewing the canon as essentially paradigms of the verbs of God's works, and a putative paradigm suggesting the verbs of our works in the light of God's, issues in a theocentric perspective on the Bible. It is God who is Creator, it is God who is Elector, it is God who is Redeemer, it is God who is Sustainer, it is God who is Judge and Re-creator. To focus on only one aspect of God's works, such as redemption, can issue in denominationalism and particularism: christocentrism or redemption-centered theology can issue in exclusivity, just as emphasis only on God as Creator of all the world and of all peoples can issue in a flaccid kind of universalism. A theocentric hermeneutic applied to the canon as paradigm can liberate us today both from the ancient mores reflected in the Bible which may be uncouth and from the kinds of denominationalism which always seem to crouch so close to the door of biblical interpretation.

If one is willing to admit that the gospel starts with God's works in Genesis, and if one is willing to refrain from moralizing while reading the Bible through, one can keep asking episode after episode and century after century in biblical history (story) what it says God was doing. And out of the answers comes a paradigm of the way God speaks, thinks, and acts in all kinds of different contexts in antiquity, including the New Testament. For what God does there is essentially what he had been doing from the start. The difference was not in God's acts; the difference was essentially in the cultural context and idiom in which the act or speech was reported. From this one gets an impression of how God might be acting in the contexts of today—dynamically, not statically.

A number of results ensue. One sees the continuity between the Testaments much more clearly than by other modes of reading the Bible. One does not overstress the human agents God uses along the way, or the created conditions, or the various mores of the various cultures of the ancient Near East, but how God worked in and through and often despite them to weave his own story. *Errore hominum providentia divina.* The point of the annunciation stories in Luke chapter 1 is not that Elizabeth was old and barren or that Mary was young and virginal. The point is the statement of Gabriel at the climax of the accounts: "With God nothing is impossible" (Luke 1:38; cf. in the Septuagint Gen. 18:14). The point, as Luke stressed, is what God was doing opening the wombs of the two women (as he had earlier done with Old Testament matriarchs)—not the condition of the women. To stress biblical mores or customs or agents can be to miss the point altogether.

Other results are a liberation from the hermeneutics of evolutionism, the tacit assumption that what is later in the Bible is somehow better; a liberation from the anti-Semitic hermeneutic that has so crippled Christianity and brought pain to the heart of God, not to speak of suffering to Jews; a renewed conviction that the New Testament, despite its odd Greek and hellenistic idioms, is also biblical and belongs in the canon (even though it is quite late and quite scandalous in its claims); the empowering good news that God reveals his Christ to the world rather than that Christ somehow at that late date revealed God to the world (where did such a notion get started anyway?). The same God is the subject of the verbs of the New Testament gospel as of the verbs of the Old Testament gospel. And the Bible as canon presents paradigms on how to conjugate those verbs—if read by the hermeneutics discernible in the Bible itself, some of which we have attempted to employ here.

What would one such paradigm derived from the Bible look and sound like? There are surely numerous possibilities, one of which can be suggested here. The Torah-Christ story of the Bible, if one focuses on God's part in it, might be called a divine odyssey. Viewed from this aspect and recited in a kind of Green Pastures or Clarence Jordan idiom it would run as follows:

God, after creating the world, suffering heart pangs of his own because of human stupidity of heart, starting afresh with Noah's family, and sorting out the nations of Babel, paid a call on one Abram, a migrant laborer up in Ur, Babylonia. After chatting a while about his troubles with some rather overly brilliant members of the heavenly council, and how some day he was just going to have to cut down on all this traveling around the world, God suggested to Abram the kind of agenda he had in mind for setting things back to rights between himself and humanity—somehow to bring the human will into closer harmony with his own divine will. Humans seem apt to make a god of most anything that comes to hand, especially the works of their own hands and their own limited little visions. Anyway, he asked Abe if he would strike out on a journey with him to a place unknown to Abram. The migrant laborer agreed and he and his wife, Sarai, set out. God told him if he would sever his relations with his ancestry up there in Mesopotamia, snip his name off the family tree as it were, God would make it up to him by making Abram himself the father and progenitor of a family to come after him the likes of which you just couldn't wrap your imagination around. But, and he made this quite clear sitting right there in Abram's parlor in Ur, Abram and his family to come after him would have one overriding purpose on earth: to be an instrument for God's blessing all the other families and nations on earth—as God himself chose and saw fit. This, you see, was and is God's hidden agenda behind all this talk about election. Abram accepted the conditions and he and Sarai packed a light lunch and made their way out of town, not knowing whither they were going.

Now mind you, in this view of things God is the principal actor and agent. It is *his* plan and will being worked out. He goes with Abe and Sarai down to Shechem in Palestine, then down to Egypt and back (where they had a really narrow escape), then he picks up with the next generation, Isaac (but only after he had made quite sure one day on Mt. Moriah that Abraham really understood what was going on in the real world and what this business of having a future for the church really meant). Abraham mighty near had to sacrifice the whole idea of a future for the church in order to get it clear in his own mind why there was one in the first place. Then the divine odyssey continues with Jacob and his twelve sons, and Joseph down in Egypt. Then God stays with them even when they are made slaves down there, and he goes traipsing around until he finds Moses one day over in Midian County and gets him to go to the slaves with the message that God was to free them from slavery.

And he does, too. God had to harden Pharaoh's heart to get the slaves to see the point of the whole thing, but he got them out of there and across the Reed Sea down along the Gulf of Suez and out over the Mitla Pass down to Mt. Sinai. He ran ahead of them, got up on the mountain, and turned around just in time to welcome them and say howdy! It was there and then that he wanted to bless them beyond all imagination and give them all the secrets of lifestyle and the whole business. He got Moses to write all this down on clay tablets to give them. You see, God was so full of love for these refugee slaves that he was willing in that giddy frame of mind to tell them exactly what his will for them was. He wanted to bridge the gap right then and there (between his heart and theirs) and let them in on the way to bring the human will in close harmony to cosmic reality, to the divine will. It was such a wonderful moment that there was some thunder and lightning and I don't know what all: God was so happy he could just about burst wide open. He was willing to spell it all out right there on those tablets. And he did, too. Except that by the time Moses had put his stylus and other writing materials away and made his way back down the steep path, the whole lot of them had made themselves a god, a lot of bull really, but they just couldn't stand being all that time without some kind of a god; so they just made one. That was quite a scene, and Moses was very upset, and it made God sad.

But anyway, to make a long story short, they finally left Sinai and moseyed around through the desert there for some forty-odd years, God with them the whole time, still happy—'cause you can't get him down, really. He would show up in a pillar of fire long about bedtime and then the next morning before breakfast in a column of smoke, and he would often dash on out three days' journey ahead of them looking for watering places for them. He didn't mind this kind of running around because he knew he was really doing a righteousness and bringing salvation to the whole world without violating human will. So God was happy. And he went on with them till they got to Shittim.

Now Shittim was just a watering hole really, but that's where Moses pitched camp the last time on the east bank of the Jordan River. So, along with all the other folks, God listened to Moses' intolerably long sermon there (most of the book of Deuteronomy) and then told Moses he'd best take his ease, and Joshua could pick up at this point. Mind you, the story is about God's odyssey. He had different people accompany him as the generations went by, but the story is really about God.

So, God crossed on over the Jordan and was with Joshua and the league of families and clans that sort of liberated the Canaanite city-states. And then finally after Samuel had done what he could for the tribes, God decided he'd best have another leader. First he picked Saul to manage the threat from the Sea Peoples, who had come to Palestine from islands off to the west, and the Philistines and others, and then finally he got Samuel to pick David; and David consolidated the whole venture and went up and took Jerusalem without firing a shot (2 Samuel 5). And that pleased God so much, word has it he just about danced a jig around the walls of Jerusalem.

Now you see, that's about as far as the Old Testament Torah story gets, even in its longest form. Foreign armies conquer and unconquer and come and go and Jerusalem is destroyed a couple of times and rebuilt and all that, but the longest form of the Torah story (J account) takes the divine odyssey just to the point of entering and settling Jerusalem.

Now some people wanted to add to the Torah story back in Old Testament times. Jeremiah twice (Jer. 16:14–15 and 31:31–34) said he was quite sure that the events of his day about the destruction of Jerusalem and God's regathering the exiles would be added like another chapter to the Torah story. Ezekiel was quite sure of it; so also was Second Isaiah (Isaiah 43, e.g.) shortly thereafter. But actually they were wrong: the final edition of the basic Torah itself includes only the parts up to Moses' long sermon on the east bank of the Jordan (Genesis to Deuteronomy). That was so that Jews, if they happened to be scattered all over tarnation, wouldn't feel they had to change off and become something else just because they weren't living in Palestine. And that's one reason I'm sure Judaism has lasted so long, these twenty-five hundred years—because the basic Torah, the Pentateuch, in effect says that if you happen to be wandering and in dispersion like Abraham, Jacob, Moses, and the rest, you don't have to fret about not being on a particular piece of real estate to be identified with the people God chose to bless the whole world, and you for sure don't have to assimilate to the dominant culture where you live.

Nobody succeeded in adding a chapter to the basic Torah story —until, that's right, until the New Testament, and even then not for most Jews. Now what we can see from the point of view of the divine odyssey is that the New Testament really makes this quite bold and scandalous claim that in Christ God committed another salvation or righteousness and that it should be added to the Torah story as a climax, as the ultimate chapter of the whole story or odyssey. To put it another way, while the arguments and debates in the churches of the second century A.D. spurred by the heretic Marcion were on the point of whether or not the Old Testament was biblical, the great concern of the whole early church of the first century (including most of the New Testament writers) was to try to show that the New Testament Christ story was biblical. Now, most of Judaism said no.

But the argument of the New Testament and the early church was that God's divine odyssey did not stop with David in Jerusalem. In rhetorical terms they put it this way: If God could go with Abram from Ur of Chaldees to Palestine, down to Egypt, out of Egypt with a motley crew of refugee slaves, through the desert, conquer Palestine with Joshua, and take Jerusalem with David—why not Bethlehem? After all, it's only five miles down there out the Jaffa Gate on the old road that runs by Rachel's Tomb. If God could go all the way from Ur to Jerusalem by way of Egypt and the Sinai desert, don't you suppose he could make it another five miles down to Bethlehem? And if he was with Joseph in prison and granted his presence in the huts and hovels of slaves in Egypt with Moses, don't you reckon he could crouch down into the cradle of a Jew baby in Bethlehem, if he was of a mind? And if Pharaoh's armies didn't put him off when he pursued his agenda to free those slaves, do you suppose he would be offended by Herod's sword waging the peace in a little village by killing all those baby boys in Bethlehem?

The point would be that you just don't know what God's already been through if you think he couldn't get into that cradle in Bethlehem and onto that cross on Golgotha—and roll a stone away from a tomb, for that matter, if it was his mind to do so and on his agenda to bring righteousness and salvation to the world in that way.

Notes

1. It is very encouraging to see this point emphasized so clearly by Leander E. Keck in *The Bible in the Pulpit: The Renewal of Biblical Preaching* (Nashville: Abingdon Press, 1978), especially pp. 100–105.

2. For a review of the problem of Paul and the Law with perhaps a fresh suggestion about it see James A. Sanders, "Torah and Paul," in *God's Christ and His People* (Oslo: Universitetsforlaget, 1977), pp. 132–40.

INDEX

Index of Scriptural Passages